History of Cambodia

An Enthralling Overview from the Angkor Empire to Now

© Copyright 2025 - All rights reserved.

The content contained within this book may not be reproduced, duplicated, or transmitted without direct written permission from the author or the publisher.

Under no circumstances will any blame or legal responsibility be held against the publisher, or author, for any damages, reparation, or monetary loss due to the information contained within this book, either directly or indirectly.

Legal Notice:

This book is copyright protected. It is only for personal use. You cannot amend, distribute, sell, use, quote, or paraphrase any part, or the content within this book, without the consent of the author or publisher.

Disclaimer Notice:

Please note the information contained within this document is for educational and entertainment purposes only. All effort has been executed to present accurate, up-to-date, reliable, and complete information. No warranties of any kind are declared or implied. Readers acknowledge that the author is not engaging in the rendering of legal, financial, medical, or professional advice. The content within this book has been derived from various sources. Please consult a licensed professional before attempting any techniques outlined in this book.

By reading this document, the reader agrees that under no circumstances is the author responsible for any losses, direct or indirect, that are incurred as a result of the use of the information contained within this document, including, but not limited to, errors, omissions, or inaccuracies.

Free limited time bonus

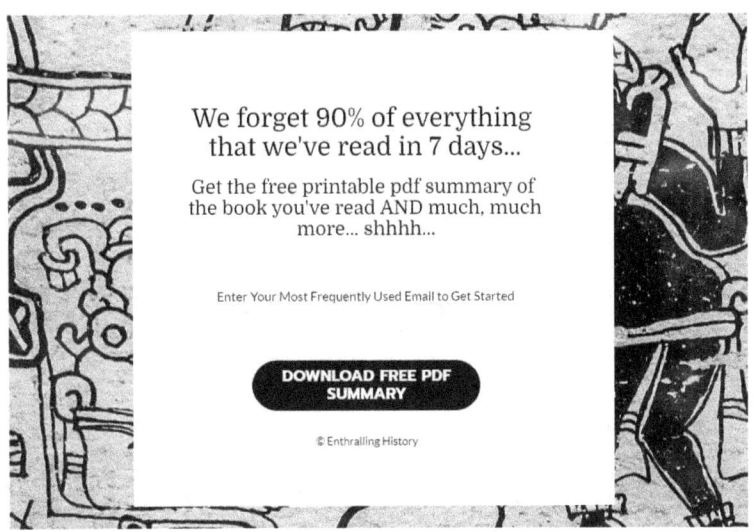

Stop for a moment. We have a free bonus set up for you. The problem is this: we forget 90% of everything that we read after 7 days. Crazy fact, right? Here's the solution: we've created a printable, 1-page pdf summary for this book that you're reading now. All you have to do to get your free pdf summary is to go to the following website:
https://livetolearn.lpages.co/enthrallinghistory/

Or, Scan the QR code!

Once you do, it will be intuitive. Enjoy, and thank you!

Table of Contents

INTRODUCTION 1
CHAPTER 1 - THE RISE OF ANGKOR 2
CHAPTER 2 - THE FALL OF ANGKOR AND THE DARK AGES ...12
CHAPTER 3 - THE PROTECTORATE OF CAMBODIA....................24
CHAPTER 4 - INDEPENDENCE AND NORODOM SIHANOUK'S REIGN 32
CHAPTER 5 - THE KHMER REPUBLIC AND CIVIL UNREST 41
CHAPTER 6 - THE KHMER ROUGE ERA: DEMOCRATIC KAMPUCHEA'S TRAGEDY 51
CHAPTER 7 - VIETNAMESE OCCUPATION AND THE PEOPLE'S REPUBLIC OF KAMPUCHEA 66
CHAPTER 8 – CAMBODIA'S TRANSITION TO PEACE: THE UNTAC MISSION AND RESTORATION OF THE MONARCHY....77
CHAPTER 9 - RECONSTRUCTION AND PROGRESS IN THE TWENTY-FIRST CENTURY 88
CONCLUSION 98
HERE'S ANOTHER BOOK BY ENTHRALLING HISTORY THAT YOU MIGHT LIKE..100
FREE LIMITED TIME BONUS..101
BIBLIOGRAPHY 102
IMAGE SOURCES 108

Introduction

China's size and population make it the primary area of study for many historians when it comes to Eastern countries. However, this does not mean that other countries in the East did not contribute to the historical record and culture of the area. Other nations played prominent roles, and one whose impact on history and culture was much more significant than its landmass or demographics is Cambodia.

This tiny nation in Southeast Asia has an incredible history of resilience. Cambodia flourished under the Khmer Empire, with Angkor Wat standing as a testament to its power and influence. Despite the profound suffering inflicted by the Pol Pot regime in the 20th century, Cambodia has emerged as an aspiring nation with a promising future. Its legacy and the strength of its people are not to be overlooked.

This book is dedicated to providing a thorough and honest portrayal of Cambodia and the history it has shaped. From the early years before the Khmer Empire to the present day, we will delve into the nation's significant transformations, including periods of human disasters. Despite the challenges that originally looked insurmountable, Cambodia has picked itself up, and its past, present, and future can be described as nothing short of glorious.

Chapter 1 - The Rise of Angkor

Significant civilizations have developed along the banks of great rivers. This was true in Egypt, whose culture was influenced by the Nile, and Babylonia, with its access to the Tigris and Euphrates Rivers. The dominant river in Southeast Asia is the Mekong. This waterway has influenced the creation of human settlements in Myanmar, Laos, Thailand, Vietnam, and Cambodia.

Cambodia owes much of its history to the Mekong River. For millennia, this river provided the water necessary for agriculture and served as a vital transportation route from the northeast to the southwest. The annual flooding that determines rice cultivation in Cambodia, as well as the potential catastrophe caused by a drought, all underscore the crucial role of the Mekong River in enabling the people of Cambodia to live and thrive.

Early Kingdoms

We know from historical records and archaeological excavations about two kingdoms in what is now Cambodia during the 1st millennium of the Common Era. The Funan Kingdom existed from the 1st to the 6th century CE. This kingdom was located in the Mekong Delta, and it served as a vital link in the trade between China and India. Indian influence was considerable, and the Hindu religion was prominent. The Funan Kingdom had both an advanced urban culture and a highly productive farming area. Its infrastructure included roads and canals, which added to the kingdom's prosperity. Other kingdoms noted the abundance of food Funan had. Even the Chinese were impressed by

Funan's treasure and luxury. Its position as an international trade center allowed it to retain influence for several centuries.

Funan was torn apart by internal civil dissent and eventually was absorbed by the Kingdom of Chenla, which had once been a vassal state of China. This state rose to power in the 6th century CE. While Funan was concentrated primarily on the coast, Chenla was more inland, and its economy focused on rice agriculture and the control of land trade routes. It was not a centralized state, and there were two regions: Land Chenla and Water Chenla (the former was more concerned with farming, and the latter's greater interest was commerce with foreigners).

Yet, Cambodia's new state was still a significant commercial cog in the international economy of Southeast Asia. Both of these kingdoms were instrumental in spreading Hindu culture and Indian ideas. Indian beliefs regarding jurisprudence, literature, astronomy, and the use of Sanskrit permeated both societies.[i]

The Indian concept of kingship had a strong influence on both kingdoms. The concept of divine kingship, in which the king was perceived as either a god or the representative of the gods on earth, was accepted in the region. Rituals, particularly the Vedic ceremonies, were part of the royal ceremonies of both Cambodian kingdoms. Although one would think that the proximity to China would allow the Chinese to have greater control over these Cambodian kingdoms' culture and customs, India was the primary social and political model.

Both kingdoms did admirable things and left a record that showed significant achievements. However, whatever they did paled in comparison to what would come next. Cambodia would be the site of one of the major empires of the civilized world.

---

[i] Factsanddeteails.com. (2024, December 1). *Ancient Civilizations in Cambodia: Funan and Champa and the Chams*. Retrieved from FactsandDetails.com:
https://factsanddetails.com/southeast-asia/Cambodia/sub5_2a/entry-2839.html

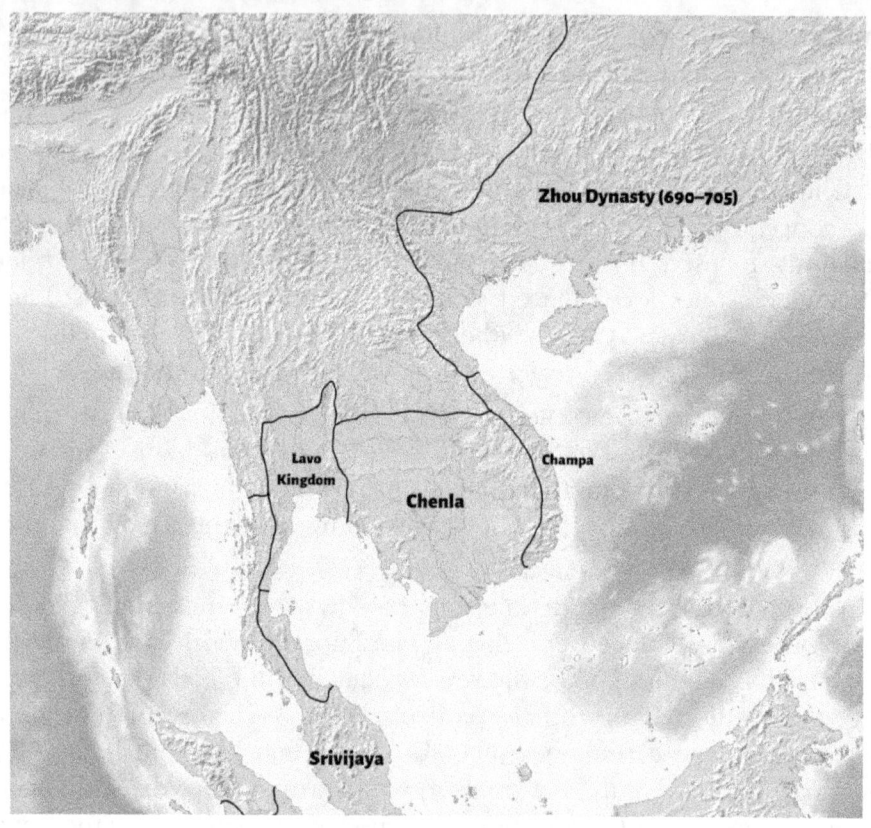
Chenla in 700 CE.[1]

Decline of Chenla

Chenla's lack of internal unity led to severe problems. The country did not have a strong monarchy, which led to political destabilization as rivals fought for control of the country. External pressures were also bearing down on the kingdom. Champa, a kingdom in present-day Vietnam to the east, and the Dvaravati Kingdom of Siam (today's Thailand) to the west threatened this Cambodian nation on two fronts. Chenla suffered from a shift in traditional maritime trade routes, which made it difficult for the kingdom to finance necessary defenses.

Water Chenla had to contend with numerous pirate attacks and incursions from Java, Sumatra, and other Southeast Asian areas. The Shailendra dynasty of Java finally brought the coastal region to its knees. Water Chenla was reduced to becoming a vassal state of that foreign power. The final nail in the coffin occurred when the last Water Chenla king was killed, and the kingdom became part of the Javanese kingdom in 790 CE.

Land Chenla was reasonably secure because it was located in the interior, but the Khmer people, the predominant population of Chenla, had to accept the idea of a foreign power controlling the coastal area. That was an intolerable situation that needed an immediate remedy.

The Universal Monarch

Uniting a divided country often requires a charismatic person capable of drawing others and providing a sense of purpose to them. Jayavarman II was such a person. He is credited with founding a nation that would stamp its image on Southeast Asian history.

The historical record is cloudy, but we can gather that Jayavarman was installed on the throne of Water Chenla as a vassal for the Javanese. He was a willing subordinate until 802. He then declared himself the universal monarch, or Chakravartin, in a ceremony on Phnom Kulen, a mountain range, that year.

Jayaraman did more than go through the motions of proclaiming himself a monarch; he backed it up with military force. He conducted military campaigns within Cambodia and against the Javanese. He used the Hindu religion as a means of consolidating his power. Jayaraman encouraged a god-king cult (*Devaraja*) to develop and grow into a belief system that legitimized his temporal and spiritual authority. His actions amounted to a declaration of independence from the Javanese. Jayaraman II is credited with ending Javanese dominance over Cambodia.

The universal monarch was busy solidifying his gains and guaranteeing that the new political entity would survive long after he died. Jayavarman II consolidated local states into a single kingdom, appointing regional governors to administer their territories. However, the extent of administrative reform under his rule remains unclear; governance likely varied by region and was shaped more by ritual authority than centralized bureaucracy. Still, Jayavarman was able to pass on the legacy of a unified state to his heirs.

He is credited with having founded the city of Hariharalaya. This urban center was one of the first Khmer capitals and was located in the Angkor region. Although there is no temple officially credited to Jayavarman, his construction efforts might have been the beginning of what would become the largest temple complex in Asia.

Jayavarman was not the only architect of the rise of the Khmer Empire, but he played a significant role in creating a national Khmer identity. Hindu customs and practices were being deeply integrated into the social identity of the Khmer people, and Jayavarman II inserted the idea of divine kingship into the national awareness of the people. Overthrowing the Javanese overlord was the ultimate step in Jayavarman's cultural awareness efforts. The foreigners were no longer in control; the Khmers would decide Cambodia's future destiny.

The Khmer Empire, at its peak, encompassed Cambodia and parts of Thailand, Laos, Vietnam, and Myanmar. Provinces were governed by appointed officials who reported to centralized authorities, and these local magistrates were responsible for tax collection and maintaining order. There was a law code that helped with administration and a standing army to enforce any government missives.

The Khmer Social Order

Each stratum of society had its role to play. The god-king was the supreme ruler, and his divinity was constantly reinforced through ceremonies and customs. The nobility were not idle. Their role was to govern the empire as administrators and guarantee that the king's authority was not challenged. Priests have always had a significant role to play in Hindu culture, and this was also true in the Khmer Empire. Hindu and Buddhist practices were instilled in the people through the activity of the local clergy.

The skilled workers were responsible for creating the magnificent works of art and architecture that visitors to Cambodia can still find today. The peasants, although low in the hierarchical structure, played a significant role in agriculture, which depended on labor-intensive rice cultivation. These people would also be involved in the public works projects that the god-king would authorize. Finally, there were the slaves. They provided hard labor. They were either prisoners of war or had been sold into slavery to pay off debts.[i]

Indianization

The influence of Indian culture was pervasive, but was it oppressive? The subcontinent has been plagued for millennia by the caste system, which forced people into social positions. Was there a comparable caste system in the Khmer Empire?

---

[i] Jojo. (2024, December 1). *Social Structure*. Retrieved from Angkorempiretj.weebly.com: https://angkorempiretj.weebly.com/social-structure.html

The answer is no. The Khmers might have been influenced by the Indian culture, but this did not mean that every aspect of the Indian belief system was incorporated into Khmer society.

Contact with India was not the result of a conquering army or the persuasive preaching of a Brahmin mystic. Contact with India was primarily through trade. Commercial opportunities encouraged Indian merchants to immigrate to Cambodia, where they intermarried and introduced Indian customs to the local population. However, what the Khmers and other people of Southeast Asia had was a form of cultural borrowing: they adopted what they liked and ignored the rest. The Khmer people might have worshiped Hindu gods, but the caste system and Hindu dietary habits were not necessarily included. Moreover, there was no discernible allegiance to India. It was not viewed as a motherland.[i]

The Presence of the Buddha

Hinduism was not the only religion that influenced Khmer society. There was another central belief system that was imported from India: Buddhism. Its introduction to Cambodia came in the 3rd century BCE, and Buddhism became prominent in the 5th century CE. The Buddhist moral code, which emphasized honesty, nonviolence, and caring for others, appealed to the ordinary people of Cambodia and provided a way to structure a life that could govern daily interactions. Buddhism also encouraged community service. Buddhist monks provided medical care and various social services to the people.

During the reign of King Jayavarman VII, Buddhism became a significant presence in Khmer society. The king converted to Mahayana Buddhism and made it the state religion. Mahayana Buddhism emphasizes bodhisattvas—enlightened beings who assist others on the path to enlightenment—and often features richly symbolic and elaborate artistic expressions. Its influence is visible in the architecture and iconography of Khmer temples from the period.

Over time, Theravada Buddhism became the predominant form of the religion in Cambodia. Unlike Mahayana, Theravada Buddhism focuses more on individual enlightenment through personal discipline and meditation, and its practices are generally simpler. Its primary text is

---

[i] Kalyanaraman, S. (2018). *Processes of Indianization in the Khmer Empire.* Retrieved from Angkordatabase.asia: https://angkordatabase.asia/publications/processes-of-indianization-in-the-khmer-empire

the Pali Canon, which includes monastic rules, teachings of the Buddha, and philosophical analysis. Buddhist monasteries and temples were educational centers, and the religion would play a dominant role in the construction projects of the Khmer civilization.[i]

Watering the Land

The Khmer Empire required large-scale food production to sustain its hundreds of thousands of people. Thanks to the highly sophisticated irrigation system that was implemented, the Khmer people were able to grow bumper crops of rice and other foodstuffs.

A baray is a reservoir constructed to hold substantial amounts of water. Khmers constructed these large water storage facilities to help farmers during the dry season. Water was distributed through a canal system that moved this valuable resource from the barays to the fields. Water flow was controlled through dikes and spillways, which guaranteed a consistent and manageable amount of water for agricultural use.

Terracing was an important part of farming, and terraces were used for rice cultivation. The best example of Khmer water management can be found at Angkor. The reservoir system that was constructed initially permitted control of water during times of flooding and drought. The West Baray, which was estimated to have been sixteen square kilometers and held billions of gallons of water, is still capable of storing water today.[ii]

The Temple Builders

The national flag of Cambodia is the only flag with a temple in its center. This alone underscores the importance of temples in the Khmer Empire. Numerous temples were constructed before the advent of the Khmer Empire, but the primary period of construction took place from the late 9th century into the early 13th century.

The Khmers were influenced by Indian temple architecture, but a distinct style developed in Cambodia. Khmer architecture, known as Angkorian, had some unique features. The Khmer temples are enclosed by a concentric series of walls with the central sanctuary in the center. A

---

[i] Ibcworld.org. (2024, December 1). *Buddhism Around the World*. Retrieved from Ibcworld.org: https://www.ibcworld.org/home/diaspora/Cambodia.

[ii] lwmays. (2015, May 21). *Water Technologies of the Khmer Civilization: Angkor*. Retrieved from Ancientwatertechnologies.com: https://ancientwatertechnologies.com/2015/05/21/water-technologies-of-the-khmer-civilization-angkor/.

gallery passageway runs along the enclosure, and the entrance building, known as a gopura, can be found at the four cardinal points of a temple. The temples constructed during King Jayavarman VII's reign (r. 1181-1218) featured a hall of dancers. This was a building divided into four courtyards by galleries. A house of fire (Dharmasala) was a building only found in temple constructions; these were either rest places for travelers or the repository of sacred flame.

A house of fire at Preah Khan.[a]

The temple complex of Angkor Wat best exemplifies Angkorian architecture. Angkor Wat is intended to be a representation of the home of the Hindu gods, Mount Meru. The moat that surrounds Angkor Wat is intended to symbolize the waters that surround that holy mountain. The central tower, which is the peak of Mount Meru, is surrounded by smaller towers, and bas-reliefs that depict Hindu themes can be found on the walls.

Indeed, narrative themes can be found everywhere in Khmer temples, and the towers themselves were shaped in the form of lotus buds to suggest spiritual enlightenment. Broad passageways are also a feature of Angkorian architecture.[i] Sandstone was a principal building

---

[i] Agatetravel.com. (2024, December 1). *Angkor Wat Architecture.* Retrieved from Agatetravel.com: https://www.agatetravel.com/angkor-wat-architecture.html

stone and was easily obtained from Phnom Kulen.

The Principal Temples

Angkor Wat is the Khmer temple that stands out the most. It was constructed in the late 11th and 12th centuries, initially beginning during King Suryavarman II's reign (r. 1113-1150).

Jayavarman VII was the builder king of the Khmers. Several noteworthy temples were constructed during his reign, and their ruins are still being explored by archaeologists to understand more about the Khmer people.

- Bayon

    Bayon was erected in the last capital of the Khmer Empire, Angkor Thom, and it was the last complex temple built by the king. Bayon is a three-tiered pyramid temple with a high tower topped by four gigantic carved faces that some scholars believe are copies of Jayavarman's face. In total, more than two thousand large faces are carved in this building complex. While smaller than Angkor Wat, Bayon's features include the outer galleries that depict battles between the Khmer and their enemies. The other galleries also display scenes of daily life that give us an idea of the lives of ordinary people.[i]

- Preah Khan

    Preah Khan means "sacred sword" in Khmer, and the king built it in honor of his father, Dharanindravarman II (r. 1150-1160). It was more than just a place of holy worship. The temple complex served as a monastery and a university. The Preah Khan stele records how many people it required to maintain this property: nearly 100,000 Prajnaparamita men and women kept Preah Khan operating.[ii]

- Banteay Kdei

    Banteay Kdei was meant to be a monastic complex. It was used by monks until the 1960s. It was a triad temple with three deities: Lokesvara, representing compassion; Prajnaparamita, a female divinity of wisdom; and the Buddha. Various statues and artwork

---

[i] Varro, L. (2024, December 1). *Bayon Temple*. Retrieved from Lucasvarro.com: https://lucasvarro.com/blogs/angkorpedia/bayon-temple

[ii] Varro, L. (2024, December 1). *Preah Jhan Temple*. Retrieved from Lucasvarro.com: https://lucasvarro.com/blogs/angkorpedia/preah-khan-temple

displaying the traditions of various Buddhist sects and Hinduism showcase the king's wish to promote religious harmony.[i]

There were a number of reasons for building these temples besides sincere religious devotion. The Khmer temples were massive public works projects requiring a large workforce and a service population to keep the buildings functional. The temples also provided forums for cultural and social events that brought communities together and unified the population. These temples were part of large-scale urban planning activities that helped the economy of the Khmer Empire and provided a cultural legacy that remains to this day.

---

[i] Sailingstonetravel.com. (2018, December 26). *The Mysteries of Jayavarman VII's Triad Temples*. Retrieved from Sailingstone.com: https://sailingstonetravel.com/jayavarman-viis-triad-temples/

Chapter 2 - The Fall of Angkor and the Dark Ages

The Superpower

The Khmer Empire was the preeminent country in Southeast Asia for centuries. It began to expand once the centralization process was complete. The Khmers were able to subjugate various tribes and ethnic groups, maintaining control for generations.

The Khmer Empire's expansion was significantly aided by its formidable military force. Its well-organized army was equipped with a variety of weapons, including war elephants. With this army, the empire was able to conquer any opposing force. The internal difficulties of the Chinese Song dynasty (960-1279) and the threat of the Mongols provided a strategic opportunity for expansion. With China's attention diverted, the Khmer Empire could expand its territory without fear of intervention.[i]

Suryavarman II (r. 1113-1150) led military campaigns against the Vietnamese Kingdom of Champa but was not very successful. He had better luck with his efforts in modern-day Thailand and Laos. Jayavarman VII succeeded against Champa and extended Khmer territory into Vietnam, Thailand, and Laos. The diplomatic efforts of

---

[i] World History EDU. (2024, May 26). *History & Major Facts About the Khmer Empire.* Retrieved from Worldhistoryedu.com: https://worldhistoryedu.com/history-major-facts-about-the-khmer-empire/

both monarchs were reasonably successful. Suryavarman interacted with the Chola dynasty of southern India. Jayavarman, on the other hand, developed a network of tributary states along the Khmer border, creating strategic networks that could be buffer zones.

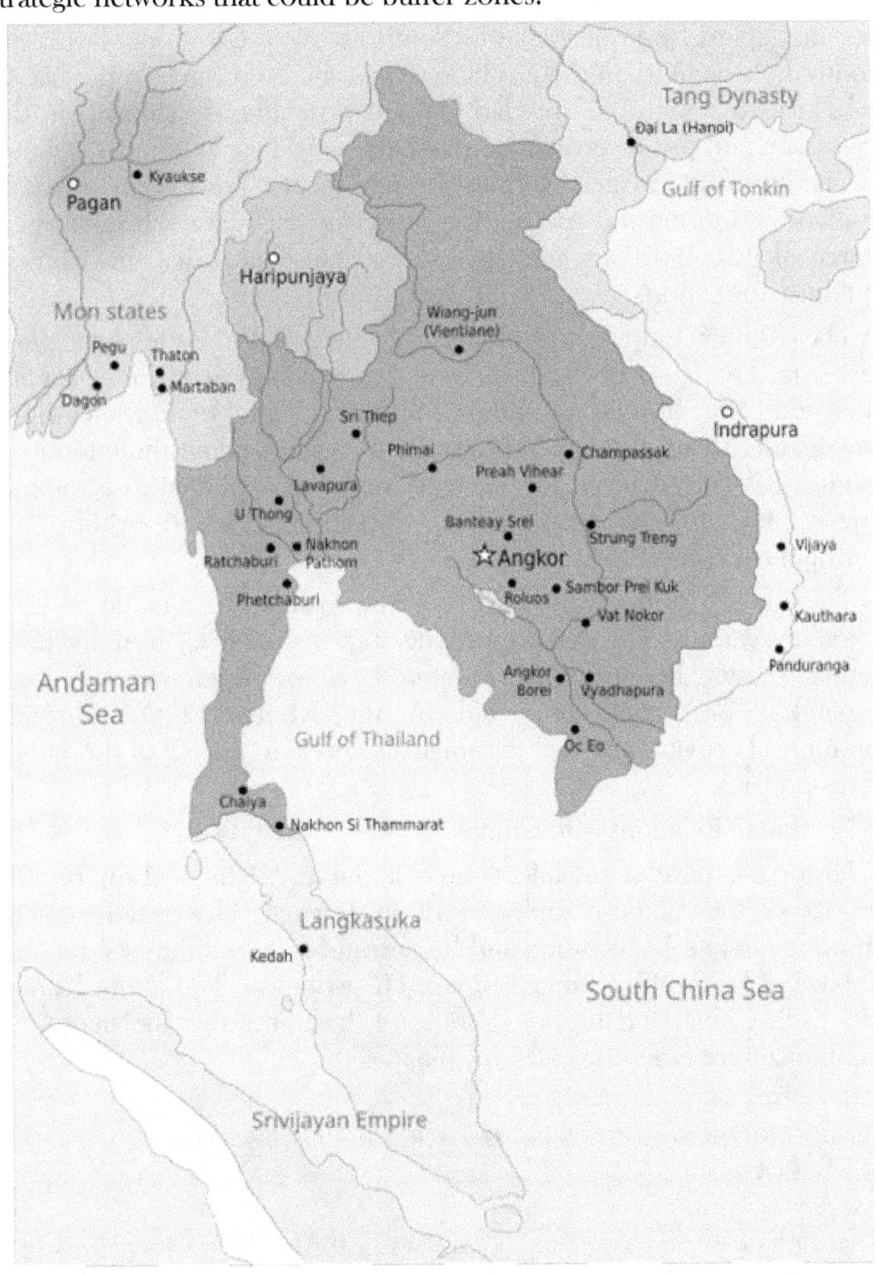

The Khmer Empire around 900 CE.[8]

Economic Dominance

The superiority of Khmer hydraulic engineering cannot be overstated. The sophisticated water management the Khmer used permitted them to exploit the waters of the Mekong River and Tonle Sap, the largest freshwater lake in Southeast Asia. Cambodia has a six-month dry season when there is little to no rain. Nevertheless, the barays and canals that were constructed allowed agriculture to flourish in the dry season and produce multiple rice harvests. These bumper crops fed the people and created surpluses for export. Tonle Sap expands dramatically during the monsoon season and has always been a great source of fish. Both rice and fish were commodities that the Khmers could use for exports.

The Khmer Empire was strategically located for trade throughout East Asia. The Khmers were able to use trade routes that headed toward India and China to their advantage. Moreover, inland trade routes along the Mekong River permitted commerce to reach far into the interior of Southeast Asia. Urban centers such as Angkor contributed to economic growth due to the commercial workshops located within the metropolitan areas.[i]

The Khmer Empire was a source of raw materials that could be used by other nations. The forests produced items such as bird feathers, elephant tusks, beeswax, and rosewood, all of which were in great demand.[ii] The wealth generated by the Khmer Empire through commercial activity provided the finances necessary for all of the public works projects.

Economic Relations with China

Historians have a reliable source about the Khmer Empire: the writings of the Chinese diplomat Zhou Daguan. He visited Angkor Thom in the late 13th century, and his account is one of the best records we have of life in the Khmer Empire. His writings talked about Khmer trade with China, and he noted some of the things that the people of Cambodia were eager to get from China:

---

[i] oup.com. (2025, January 1). *The Khmer Empire.* Retrieved from oup.com: https://www.oup.com.au/__data/assets/pdf_file/0024/58191/Chapter-13-The-Khmer-Empire-obook-only.pdf

[ii] Khmerknowledgekeepers.weekly.com. (2025, January 1). *Welcome to the Khmer Knowledge Keepers' History of the Khmer Empire.* Retrieved from Khmerknowledgekeepers.weekly.com: https://khmerknowledgekeepers.weebly.com/key-featues-of-the-khmer-empire.html

"The people of Cambodia value items made of double-threaded silk in various colors. They also value such things as pewter ware from Zenzhou, lacquer ware dishes from Wenzhou, and celadon ware from Quanzhou."[i]

The diplomat's account indicates that there was a strong relationship between the Khmer Empire and China. Daguan's account also speaks of the monarch's splendor and the capital city's bustling atmosphere. The Khmer Empire was clearly a key player in the international world of diplomacy and trade. However, the Khmer people's ascendancy was on borrowed time when the Chinese official paid his visit.[ii]

In 1586, a Portuguese Capuchin friar by the name of Antonio da Madalena traveled to Cambodia and went inland with a few guides. They moved into the steamy jungles of Cambodia, where they came across a marvelous site. The friar was the first European to behold Angkor Wat. He was stupefied by what he saw.

Madalena was amazed at the architectural splendor of the ruins and the refinement of the design of the buildings. He believed that what he observed was a religious complex that was like no other monument in the entire world. He was able to determine that Indian themes inspired the architecture.

What is essential to understand is that the friar came upon an area that was sparsely inhabited. What used to be a metropolitan area of close to one million people was almost deserted except for a few Buddhist monks and wild animals. The religious complex that was known as Angkor Wat was little more than a ruin of what it once was.

---

[i] Library.gov.au. (2025, January 1). *The Way of Life in the Khmer Empire.* Retrieved from Library.gov.au: https://www.library.gov.au/learn/digital-classroom/angkorkhmer-empire-802-1431/way-life-khmer-empire

[ii] Library.gov.au. (2025, January 1). *The Way of Life in the Khmer Empire.* Retrieved from Library.gov.au: https://www.library.gov.au/learn/digital-classroom/angkorkhmer-empire-802-1431/way-life-khmer-empire

Angkor Wat.[4]

By the time this European arrived, the Khmer Empire had collapsed. Its fall was dramatic and happened over a period of time. There was no one reason for its demise. A number of factors gradually eroded the foundations of the empire, but there was a final act that brought everything to an end.

Internal Problems

Khmer society was tolerant, but cracks were starting to form in the stable social order. Jayavarman VII made Buddhism the state religion, but this does not mean his successors were always followers of the Buddha. Some of the succeeding rulers returned to Hinduism, and the nobility was more inclined to follow the old religion. This theological flip-flopping confused ordinary people who wondered if the monarch really was a god-king.

There was an issue of social inequality that was not being adequately addressed either. Peasants bore the brunt of taxation and were forced to work on the massive construction projects throughout the empire. This was all happening while the king and his court were living in obvious luxury, as were the priests and monks.

Theravada Buddhism

Theravada Buddhism was introduced into the Khmer Empire through trade relations with Sri Lanka in the late 13th century. One of its followers was King Indravarman (r. 1295–1308). Theravada Buddhism was the dominant religion when Zhou Daguan visited.[i]

This form of Buddhism was noted for its simplicity and emphasis on individual meditation. Instead of elaborate rituals, the individual developed a closer and more personal relationship with religious beliefs. There was a sense of community derived from this form of Buddhism because the monks depended on donations from the people, which means the sect was not tied closely to the state. Its spread to the Khmer Empire resulted in a form of social transformation, as monks were drawn not just from social elites but also from peasants.

Theravada Buddhism decentralized religious authority within the Khmer Empire. The monks began to act as a check on the power of the nobility, and the monastic community did not hesitate to criticize the powerful or base their support of the king on his proven devotion. The local emphasis of Theravada Buddhism meant that building enormous temple complexes was unnecessary. The money could be spent elsewhere, and the peasants were not required to give as much of their time to construction projects.

The egalitarian qualities of this form of Buddhism caused some tension between the haves and the have-nots in Khmer society. The first signs of internal trouble began shortly after the death of Jayavarman VII. The construction of great temples slowed to a halt, and there were few major building projects in the 13th century. The historical record suffered because of this. What we know of the Khmer Empire comes primarily from temple inscriptions; text written in palm-leaf manuscripts was perishable and disintegrated. Consequently, there are gaps in the historical accounts.

Trouble on the Border

What we do know about political events in the 13th century is that after the death of Jayavarman VII in 1218, the Khmer pulled back from provinces they had taken from Champa. There was trouble in the west, and the Thai subjects rebelled. They created the Sukhothai Kingdom and were able to force the border of the Khmer Empire to recede farther east. The Mongols under Kublai Khan posed a threat in 1283; an invasion of the Khmer Empire was only avoided through paying tribute to the Mongols.

---

[i] Newwoldencyclopedia.org. (2025, January 1). *Khmer Empire.* Retrieved from Newwoldencyclopedia.org: https://www.newworldencyclopedia.org/entry/Khmer_Empire

Thai Migration

The collapse of the Roman Empire is attributed to an inability to manage the mass migrations of Germanic peoples. The Khmer Empire faced the same problem: the migration of the Thais. These people originally lived in the Yunnan area of China. They gradually began to move southward because the Mongol military campaigns in the mid-13th century placed considerable pressure on the Thais to move to where they would be safest. The Thais ultimately began to push the Khmers back, gaining substantial territory in what is now Thailand.[i] Another Thai kingdom, Ayutthaya, was formed in 1351, and its Thai inhabitants conducted raids into Khmer territory.[ii]

There was no relief on the eastern borders either. Champa and Dai Viet, a kingdom in what is now northern Vietnam, were constantly fighting over territory in the 14th century. The expansionist goals of both kingdoms posed a constant threat to the Khmer Empire. The greatest danger, however, was not military but economic. Disputes between those two countries disrupted trade that the Khmer commanders and rulers relied on. Moreover, resources had to be diverted to the borders in the event of an incursion by either neighbor.

Environmental Issues

Academics speculate that one of the reasons for the decline of the Khmer Empire was environmental issues, which were either out of the control of the government or were not responded to effectively. The empire owed a great deal of its success to the fertility of the soil. However, that precious resource was constantly in a precarious state. Water was critical. The dry season lasted for months, and a steady supply of water was necessary to keep rice crops saturated. Any trouble with the water supply would result in disastrous consequences.

Drought was an obvious danger. Modern science allows us to investigate climate irregularities that occurred hundreds of years ago. The examination of the cross sections of ancient tree rings indicates that Angkor suffered a significant drought in the mid-14th century.[iii]

---

[i] Plubins, R. Q. (2013, March 12). *Khmer Empire*. Retrieved from Worldhistory.org: https://www.worldhistory.org/Khmer_Empire/

[ii] Library.gov.au. (2022, July 11). *The Decline of the Khmer Empire*. Retrieved from Library.gov.au: https://www.library.gov.au/learn/digital-classroom/angkorkhmer-empire-802-1431/decline-khmer-empire

[iii] Prasad, J. (2020, April 14). *Climate Change and the Collapse of Angkor Wat*. Retrieved from

The drought was not a short-term problem; it lasted for years. It decreased the nutrient-rich sediment that the rice fields depended on and caused the water levels in the reservoirs to drop. The extended drought was not ignored. There is evidence that the Khmers tried to raise the water levels of the East Baray by closing an exit canal, but that did not cause the rain to fall.

When the rain did fall, it was intense. The Khmer Empire had to endure monsoon seasons that brought down torrential amounts of rain. The overflow created floods and damaged the hydraulic infrastructure of the farming areas and the cities. The hydraulic engineering of the Khmers required constant attention and careful maintenance. That gradually began to fall off. Geoscientific research has noted that the evidence of pollen remains showed considerable swamp vegetation covering the water system of Angkor Thom. Researchers have concluded that this is evidence of essential maintenance being neglected.

Deforestation was a significant factor in the decline as well. The Khmer Empire needed land for agriculture and also required substantial quantities of timber for cooking fires and massive construction projects. A combination of soil analysis and imagery from satellites has revealed considerable deforestation. The soil slowly eroded and became less productive. The Khmers were facing an environmental disaster that was caused partly by unpredictable weather and partly by their own negligence.[i]

The economy was suffering from all of these problems. Tonle Sap was a valuable source of fish, but with declining water levels, the catch grew smaller and smaller. The Khmers were losing their financial base, which had been sustained for generations by farming and fishing. Outside political forces already threatened society, and the Khmers were losing the ability to finance a proper defense.

The challenges that the Khmer Empire faced from the late 13th to the 14th century were severe. Still, they could have successfully overcome these problems had there been a cohesive, centralized state with a population that shared a national identity and purpose. That was not the

---

Sydney.edu.au: https://www.sydney.edu.au/news-opinion/news/2020/04/14/climate-change-and-angkor-wat-collapse.html

[i] Bower, B. (2019, February 25). *Ancient Angkor's Mysterious Decline May Have Been Slow, Not Sudden*. Retrieved from Sciencenews.org: https://www.sciencenews.org/article/ancient-angkor-mysterious-decline-slow-not-sudden

situation, however. The Khmers faced internal troubles that made addressing other issues very difficult.

A significant difficulty revolved around religion. The Khmer Empire transitioned to Theravada Buddhism as the recognized state religion. This form of Buddhism was not at odds with traditional power structures because of its concentration on personal growth. There is no evidence that there were major religious disputes, but Theravada Buddhism weakened the authority of the centralized state since people became more concerned with individual improvement instead of state solidarity.[i]

An 11th-century Khmer statue of the Buddha.[ii]

---

[i] Leonard C. Overton, D. P. (2025, January 1). *The Decline of Angkor*. Retrieved from Britannica.com: https://www.britannica.com/place/Cambodia/The-decline-of-Angkor

There were quarrels over succession. Several princes would jockey for power when it came time for a new king, and the consequences of the rivalries led to an increase in episodes of political friction and civil wars. The central authority, which was once the cornerstone of the empire's success, was eroding because of these internal conflicts.

When all of the problems are viewed as a whole, the Khmer Empire was on very shaky ground in the 14th century. It would not take much for a regime change to occur. All that was required was an enemy nation that was willing to engage the Khmers for control directly.

The Coming of the Thai

Ayutthaya was a Siamese kingdom located in the Chao Phraya River Valley. Its citizens referred to themselves as Thais, and at one time, the region was part of the Khmer Empire. The gradual weakness of the empire generated an inability to effectively resist foreign incursions. This political defect gave Ayutthaya an opportunity to expand at the expense of its old master. Its eventual triumph over the Khmer Empire came in stages.

Historical records show that King Ramathibodi I of Ayutthaya seized Angkor in 1353. The occupation was short-lived, and the Khmers retook the city in 1358. A later assault in 1370 resulted in an inconclusive siege. The Khmer court was able to move to Asan and then return to Angkor a few years later. The Khmers were able to hold off Ayutthaya for over fifty years, but the empire was not able to end the external threat. The final chapter of the story happened in 1431.

Collapse of Angkor

The fall of Angkor was the climax of a war with Ayutthaya. The city was besieged for seven months until it finally fell to the invading army. Angkor was extensively sacked. The Thais took more than jewels and precious metals from the ransacked metropolis. A significant number of Khmers were brought back to Ayutthaya as captives. These prisoners of war included many artisans and craftsmen; it essentially amounted to a forced migration of artistic and cultural expertise to the victorious kingdom. These prisoners would later add to the creative development of Ayutthaya.

The sack of Angkor was a dramatic end to the Khmer Empire. There would still be a Khmer presence in Cambodia, but the magnificence of its earlier days was gone. What was once a major political power in

Southeast Asia had been reduced to a backwater, and Cambodia entered a dark age.

The idea that Angkor Wat was wholly abandoned after 1431 needs to be corrected, though. The temples were still being used, and although the city lost a substantial portion of its population, the royalty would return periodically for devotional services. However, the city had definitely lost its grandeur.

Angkor was no longer defensible. The city was vulnerable to future attacks, and the ruling class had to move. The permanent capital was moved closer to what is now Phnom Penh and into an area that was easier to defend. This meant that what was left of the bureaucracy moved at the same time. The temple complexes and palaces required a population of thousands of people to maintain. Maintaining these buildings with a dwindling staff was becoming increasingly more difficult. Moreover, it was not easy to feed those who were left. Consequently, Angkor, especially Angkor Wat, gradually deteriorated.

The Khmer people eventually established their capital at Longvek. Recent excavations suggest that there was active commercial trade between Cambodia and China, Japan, Vietnam, and Thailand. The Khmer people were moving closer to the sea in an effort to escape Thai invasions.[i]

Unfortunately, the historical record of the Cambodian dark ages is spotty. Temple construction, a source of earlier information about the Khmers, was practically nonexistent, and archives of information might have been destroyed. Oral tradition was replacing written records as a source of knowledge about Cambodia. What we do know is that the Ayutthaya Kingdom exerted substantial dominance over Cambodia. Angkor was briefly reoccupied by King Chan I (r. 1516–1566). Some of the temples were restored, and new inscriptions were created. The revival was short-lived, though, as the Thais invaded and sacked Longvek in the 1590s.[ii]

The internal politics of Cambodia had turned chaotic. Regional states were created, and there was internal strife. Christian missionaries from

---

[i] Miller, M. (2016, January 13). *New Discoveries at Ancient Cambodian Capital Dispel Old Beliefs*. Retrieved from Ancient-origins.net: https://www.ancient-origins.net/news-history-archaeology/new-discoveries-ancient-cambodian-capital-dispel-old-beliefs-005160

[ii] Leonard C. Overton, D. P. (2025, January 1). *The Decline of Angkor*. Retrieved from Britannica.com: https://www.britannica.com/place/Cambodia/The-decline-of-Angkor

Portugal and Spain established a presence in the 16th century, but their influence was minor. The economic prosperity that had been a hallmark of the Khmer Empire was severely disrupted due to constant warfare and political disintegration. The Cambodian culture survived by accepting a subservient role to Thai and Vietnamese overlords. Fortunately for Cambodia, the Thais and the Vietnamese were more concerned with other matters. By the time the European powers had developed an interest in Southeast Asia, Cambodia was just a shell of what it had once been.

Chapter 3 - The Protectorate of Cambodia

By the 18th century, the political entity once known as the Khmer Empire had faded away. While the people and culture were still Khmer, the name "Cambodia" became increasingly used, especially by foreign powers and, later, the French colonial administration. Cambodia officially became a protectorate of France in 1863 and was later incorporated into French Indochina. This was the culmination of a period of steep decline for Cambodia, and the reasons leading up to it, including French colonial policy in the 19th century, need to be explored first.

Giving Up the Land

Cambodia increasingly fell under the dominance of Siam and Vietnam in the 17th and 18th centuries. The country was reduced to being a vassal as the other two nations started to carve up the country and take land away from the Cambodians. The Cambodian monarchy was growing considerably weaker, and between 1603 and 1848, there were twenty-two Cambodian kings. Needless to say, Cambodia's neighbors took advantage of the situation. Cambodia was forced to give up control of its western provinces to Siam. The land in the Mekong Delta held by the Khmers, Kampuchea Krom, was handed over to the Vietnamese. The reign of Cambodian Ang Chan II (1802-1835) confirmed Cambodia's dependence on the Vietnamese and the Thais since Cambodia was sending tribute to both royal courts. Control of the country was going back and forth, and Cambodia had little independence to speak of. It was basically a pawn in a game of political chess between the neighboring countries.[i] Cambodia desperately needed the help of a powerful country.

French Colonial Ambitions

France lost its European empire with the fall of Napoleon, but that did not mean it had given up on its imperial ambitions. France still had an overpowering desire to have international influence, and this would come at the expense of significantly weaker countries.

With the Industrial Revolution in full swing in the 19th century, France was eager to boost its industrial growth. The untapped natural resources of the underdeveloped world, whether in Africa or Southeast Asia, were a tempting prospect. France's interest in Asia was not just strategic but also economic. The French hoped to establish plantation economies to cultivate rubber and coffee, among other commodities, and Asia, particularly Southeast Asia, was a promising territory for such ventures.

French Interest in Asia

France contemplated a presence in Asia for strategic and economic reasons. It was competing with Great Britain, which was already dominant in India and Malaya. Having a French flag flying in Southeast Asia could counterbalance British influence in the region.

Maritime trade was essential to the French economy, and there was a need for places to refuel and supply. Indochina was an obvious choice, with principal harbors in Tourane (Da Nang) and Cam Ranh Bay.

There was also the national prestige of owning a colonial empire. Napoleon III, the nephew of Napoleon Bonaparte, saw colonial rule as a means of enhancing France's position as an international power. His view was shared by the French public, which enabled him to embark on an aggressive colonial policy. France's expansion in Southeast Asia began in July 1857 with a decision to attack Vietnam.[ii]

---

[i] Chandler, D. P. (2024, July 18). *Tai and Vietnamese Hegemony*. Retrieved from Britannica.com: https://www.britannica.com/topic/history-of-Cambodia/Tai-and-Vietnamese-hegemony

[ii] William S. Turley, Gerald C. Hickey. (2024, December 3). *The Conquest of Vietnam by France*. Retrieved from Britannica.com: https://www.britannica.com/place/Vietnam/The-conquest-of-Vietnam-by-France

Norodom's Dilemma

King Norodom (r. 1860-1904) ascended the throne of Cambodia under a cloud of oppression. He was chosen as the successor to his father, Ang Duong, but the Thai and the Vietnamese were quarreling over which one would control Cambodia. A coup d'état led by Norodom's half-brother was suppressed with the help of Thai troops, but Norodom was not able to exert actual authority in his own kingdom. The French were already in southern Vietnam and were casting a covetous eye on Cambodia.

The French made a deal with Norodom. The Cambodian king needed the support of a powerful country to rectify a growing chaotic situation. The deal would be for Cambodia to become a French protectorate. France would safeguard Cambodia against outside enemies and would allow Norodom to remain as the king. However, the real power in the country would reside with a French general who would have his headquarters in Phnom Penh. France would provide military protection and control Cambodia's foreign and trade relations.

Norodom was making a deal with the devil. The French had no intention of being mere bodyguards for the Cambodian people. They had colonial and imperial designs on Cambodia. Norodom, on the other hand, needed some stability and a secure throne. Based on the given situation, it appeared his only option was to allow his country to be placed under the French umbrella. Cambodia officially became a French protectorate on August 11th, 1863.

Cambodia's European Master

European colonialism in the 19th century took a condescending attitude toward the colonial subjects. The new masters believed they had a civilizing mission to perform and that they were going to bring culture to the natives, even though in places like Cambodia, there already was a highly sophisticated and refined culture in place. The French were in that mindset as they began to take control of events in Cambodia.

Western educational methods were introduced, and French became the lingua franca (no pun intended) of official business. The old legal system that had existed for centuries was swept away and replaced by the Napoleonic Code. The export industry was enhanced by the development of rubber plantations, and the French used modern agricultural methods to profit as much as possible from the fertile soil.

There were advantages to being associated with the French. Cambodia got the border security it desperately needed. The Thais discovered they were no match for the French army in the Franco-Siamese crisis of 1893. Improvements were made in Cambodia that benefited the country as well. Cambodia was a backwater wreck and required considerable help before the French arrived. The French enhanced Cambodia's infrastructure by building better roads and railways. The most significant transportation improvement was the construction of the rail line from Phnom Penh to Battambang.

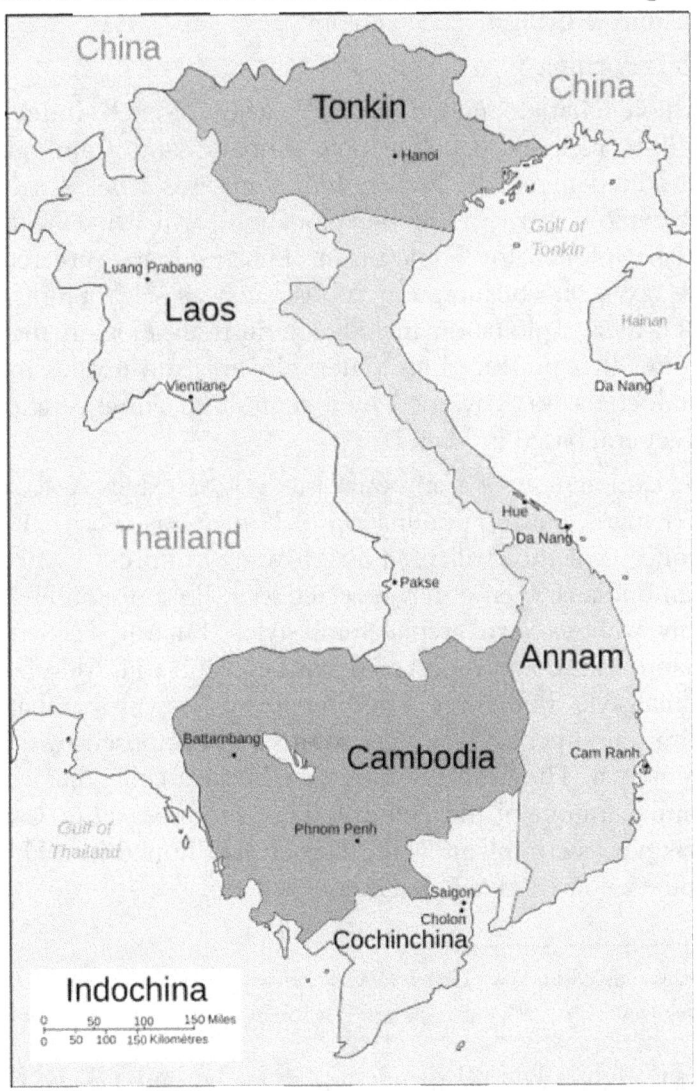

Cambodia within French Indochina. Note the two major cities of Phnom Penh and Battambang.[6]

Over time, the Cambodians discovered that being a protectorate was a mixed blessing. The country was still a kingdom, but French administrators managed almost everything in the government. The French discriminated against Cambodians, and it was obvious that real independence was nonexistent. The king was nothing more than a figurehead. The Cambodians tried to resist this foreign domination. A revolt led by King Norodom's half-brother, Si Votha, tried to expel the French in 1885 but failed. Another attempt at independence was crushed in 1886. By that time, Norodom had signed a treaty that turned Cambodia into virtually a French colony.[i]

French Indochina

The whole charade ended in 1887 when French Indochina was formed. This included Cochinchina, Annam, and Cambodia (Laos would be added in 1893). French Indochina was labeled a colony of economic exploitation (colonie d'exploitation), which meant that it was going to be exploited for French gain. The residents were required to pay heavy taxes on consumption goods, such as salt, opium, and rice alcohol. Further exploitation included industrialization in the French-built factories that produced cigarettes, alcohol, and textiles for export. French Indochina was governed by a centralized administration with a governor-general based in Hanoi.[ii]

French exploitation of Cambodia was not as extensive as what was done in Vietnam, but the domination of France was nearly stifling. The French concept of the civilizing mission was to impress French culture on the Cambodians, even if they objected to it. Phnom Penh was already an old city with its own architectural styles, but the French ignored Cambodian heritage and redesigned Phnom Penh with wide boulevards and colonial-style buildings. The intent was to prove that French architecture was superior. The education system imposed by the French was not universal. The French wanted to educate an elite that would help in the administration of the country. The minority within Cambodian society was not as compliant as the French had hoped for. They would later become a source of national consciousness.

---

[i] Factsanddetails.com. (2014, May). *French Colonial Period in Cambodia*. Retrieved from Factsanddetails.com: https://factsanddetails.com/southeast-asia/Cambodia/sub5_2a/entry-2846.html

[ii] Szczepanski, K. (2019, October 16). *What Was French Indochina?* Retrieved from ThoughtCo.com: https://www.thoughtco.com/what-was-french-indochina-195328

The Early Stirrings of Independence

The control France had over Cambodia included choosing its ruler. When King Norodom died in 1904, the French pushed his sons aside and installed Norodom's half-brother, Sisowath (r. 1904–1927), as the king. This was done because Sisowath was more cooperative with the French. An interesting feature of the control of the monarchy was the French willingness to provide complementary rations of opium to the royal family.

France did provide a psychological benefit to Cambodia. In 1907, France pressured Thailand to return lost territory to Cambodia, which resulted in Angkor being part of Cambodia once again. The French exploration of Angkor Wat provided Cambodians with a sense of national pride that, oddly enough, the French encouraged.

World War I was not just a game changer in Europe. It had a significant impact on Southeast Asia. French Indochina provided raw materials and approximately ninety-three thousand soldiers to support France during the war. When they were overseas, these soldiers were exposed to political debates and the concept of nationalism that was growing in Europe. Self-determination, something that the Indochinese had not contemplated for years, was now a topic of discussion. The Versailles Peace Conference dramatically changed the face of Europe, but the victors were not interested in changing the status quo in colonial territories. That did not stop the concept of nationalism from taking root in Asia.[i]

The Protectorate in the 1930s

The French control of Cambodia was complete in the 1930s. France was exploiting the fertile fields of the country, and rubber plantations were expanding, helping the French automobile industry. Taxation was heavy, and any development in manufacturing or infrastructure was primarily to serve the economic interests of the French colonial masters. The monarchy under King Monivong (r. 1927–1941) mainly filled ceremonial roles that maintained the loyalty of the Cambodian people, but there was no real power on the throne. French administrators made all of the major decisions in Cambodia.

---

[i] Factsanddetails.com. (2014, May). *French Colonial Period in Cambodia.* Retrieved from Factsanddetails.com: https://factsanddetails.com/southeast-asia/Cambodia/sub5_2a/entry-2846.html

Most of the resistance to the French government came from a small group of intellectuals. There was written dissent, but it was strictly censored. Although Buddhist monks showed some resistance to the French assimilation policies, it was weak. Cambodia was not much more than an afterthought and held no great importance in the grand scheme of things. There did not seem to be any possibility of change.

The Greater East Asia Co-Prosperity Sphere

Japan had a dream of reorganizing East Asia. It was called the Greater East Asia Co-Prosperity Sphere, and it was intended to dramatically change the destiny of Asia. Japan's idea would be to liberate Asia from the constraints of Western colonial administration. Asians would decide their own destiny, not the Western powers. However, what the Japanese had in mind was not entirely in the best interests of anyone but the Japanese themselves. It would be an attempt to place East Asia under the control of Japan, replacing colonial powers with a new master.[i]

Japan sincerely believed that it was meant to be the guiding force in East Asia. Its culture and mindset were superior, and Japan would lead the other Asian nations into a future shaped by the Land of the Rising Sun. The Greater East Asia Co-Prosperity Sphere would allow Japan to have access to all the raw materials East Asia had to offer. That would permit Japan to enlarge its military apparatus and control local governments through collaboration with the elites of those nations. The resources of French Indochina were greatly coveted by the Japanese government.

Japan took advantage of French setbacks in the early days of World War II and invaded French Indochina on September 22nd, 1940. The Japanese initially allowed the Vichy government to have some authority under a cooperative occupation plan, but that did not last long.

Cambodia was exploited for its agricultural products during the war. In the final days of World War II, the Japanese did something that would have enormous consequences for Cambodia. Japan declared Cambodia to be independent on March 9th, 1945. It was followed up by a declaration of independence on March 12th, 1945, by Cambodia's king, Norodom Sihanouk. The king announced at the same time that Cambodia would be referred to as Kampuchea.

---

[i] Munez, E. (2024, October 11). *Greater East Asia Co-Prosperity Sphere*. Retrieved from Britannica.com: https://www.britannica.com/topic/Greater-East-Asia-Co-prosperity-Sphere

The French Restoration

The Kingdom of Kampuchea lasted until October 1945, when the French returned and reestablished the protectorate. They hoped to restore matters to the status quo ante, which was not likely to happen. Cambodia experienced several years of no French control and had no intention of going back to the earlier days. The 1946 Constitution gave Cambodia a degree of self-government, and events in Indochina were turning against the French.

A strong sense of nationalism was growing in the area. Both Vietnamese and Cambodians were in no mood to allow the French to rule their lives anymore. Anti-French activism was gaining momentum, and leaders like Son Ngoc Thanh led the fight for self-determination. A Cambodian nationalist group known as the Khmer Issarak was organized in 1946, but it fractured before it could make any progress.

However, the French were being hit hard by the resistance growing in Vietnam. The Viet Minh, under the leadership of Ho Chi Minh and General Vo Nguyen Giap, was waging a guerrilla war in Vietnam that was draining the French. France was beginning to realize that it could no longer hang on to its colonial empire.

Chapter 4 - Independence and Norodom Sihanouk's Reign

Norodom Sihanouk became the king of Cambodia on April 24th, 1941, after his grandfather, King Sisowath Monivong, died. Sihanouk was only eighteen, and he had to carefully navigate political waters that were full of French and Japanese sharks. Amazingly, the young king proved to be a clever politician who steered his nation toward full self-determination. He was the architect of the successful transition of Cambodia from a protectorate to a sovereign nation.

Transition to Independence: The Early Days

The colonial period was over. That possibility was no longer tenable despite France's intentions of restoring the protectorate. Indochina wanted complete independence, and its nations—Vietnam, Cambodia, and Laos—expected to become fully self-governing. The Viet Minh was created as a military resistance to the Japanese and, by 1945, had hundreds of thousands of soldiers. Its leader, Ho Chi Minh, formally announced the creation of the Democratic Republic of Vietnam on September 2nd, 1945. Negotiations between the French and Viet Minh were not productive, and the First Indochina War (also known as the French War) began on December 19th, 1946.

Constitutional Changes

France was caught between a rock and a hard place. It was already fighting a war in Vietnam and did not want the conflict to engulf the rest of Indochina. While France did not want to end the protectorate, that relationship was unacceptable to the Cambodians. France had to bend a little and give more self-governance to Cambodia.

The 1946 Constitution intended to create a constitutional framework for Cambodia. Cambodia would receive a limited amount of autonomy and have a bicameral government with a National Assembly and a Council of the Kingdom. France guaranteed it had a commanding voice over the legislative process. King Sihanouk would be the ruler. If the French thought that the 1946 Constitution would solve all their problems, they were in for disappointment. The Cambodians wanted more.

The 1947 Constitution went one step beyond the original document. The National Assembly was given greater authority, and French authority was reduced. The Cambodian judiciary was given more power, and the new constitution provided explicit assurances of civil rights and liberties for Cambodian citizens. There would no longer be a pliant workforce for the French to take advantage of.

Sihanouk was willing to compromise to appease the nationalists and preserve the monarchy. The 1947 Constitution ended any appearance of an absolute monarchy. Instead, Cambodia officially became a constitutional monarchy. The 1947 Constitution was a step along the road to eventual independence. A political infrastructure was in place, and there was a constitutional monarchy that would allow for a national identity to form.

The king was showing a level of pragmatism and diplomacy beyond his years. Sihanouk was fully aware of his importance as the king, but he also knew there were players in Cambodia who were willing to take away his power if the opportunity arose. Sihanouk understood the importance of international attention, and he traveled the world to plead Cambodia's case before other nations. The Cambodian king intended to put as much pressure on the French as possible.[i]

The Royal Crusade for Independence

A combination of concern about the slow pace of ending French colonial rule and the fear that other Cambodian leaders would push him aside led the king to decide on a very bold course of action. On June 15th, 1952, Norodom Sihanouk officially made a promise to secure

---

[i] Osborne, M. (2012, October 18). *The Complex Legacy of Norodom Sihanouk*. Retrieved from Lowryinstitute.org: https://www.lowyinstitute.org/archive/complex-legacy-norodom-sihanouk

complete independence for Cambodia within three years. It was an effort to not only gain sovereign status for his country but also to leave no doubt who was in charge of the government.

The Royal Crusade for Independence started in February 1953 with a face-to-face meeting with the French president. When that did not achieve the desired results, Sihanouk traveled to Canada and the United States for support. He was able to secure interviews with influential media outlets. In these talks, the king emphasized the importance of Cambodian independence. At this time, he played his trump card.

He had an interview with Michael James, a foreign correspondent with *The New York Times*. Published on April 15th, 1953, the story warned readers that if the French rejected independence, Cambodia might seek assistance from communist China. This was the first time that the king used Cold War politics. There was a very real threat of a communist takeover in Cambodia, and that was not something Western powers wanted to see happen. France notified the Cambodians they were willing to reopen negotiations for independence eight days after that article was published.[i]

Those negotiations continued for a while longer, but the end was clearly in sight. On November 9th, 1953, Cambodia was formally granted independence from France. The colonial period in Cambodia's history was now over.

Norodom Sihanouk was the man of the hour in Cambodia. His persistence and commitment to freedom allowed Cambodia to become an independent nation. The liberation came with a whole new set of challenges for the king, though. He was very popular among the people, but there were powerbrokers in Cambodia with whom he was going to fight to determine who was going to be making the significant decisions in the newly independent country.

Opposition came from nearly everywhere and threatened the king's plans for modernizing the country. He knew that constitutional limits had been placed on the king that prohibited active participation in politics, so Sihanouk made a daring move. He abdicated on March 2nd, 1955, in favor of his father, Norodom Suramarit. This would allow

---

[i] Vachon, M. (2023, November 9). *Cambodia's Independence: What It Took to Make This Happen 70th Years Ago*. Retrieved from Cambodianess.com:
https://cambodianess.com/article/cambodias-independence-what-it-took-to-make-this-happen-70th-years-ago

Sihanouk to get directly involved with politics.

The former king created the Sangkum Reastr Niyum (the People's Socialist Community) after he stepped down. This did not mean he was stepping away from the political scene. Instead, it permitted him to become even more popular with the Cambodians. Sihanouk could use his abdication to project himself as a man of the people, one who did not care about his own personal advancement but rather the needs of every Cambodian.

His principal opponents were the Democratic Party and the Khmer Issarak. Some members of the latter were starting to become aligned with the communists. The communists were represented by the Communist Party of Kampuchea, whose members were known as the Khmer Rouge. The abdication was a brilliant move, and it enabled Sihanouk to push through initiatives in education and health services. His political party won a landslide victory in the general elections and won all of the seats in the National Assembly. This situation permitted Sihanouk to dominate the Cambodian government for years.[i]

Trouble in Indochina

The French grossly underestimated the strength of the Viet Minh. It was not a loud gang of bullies and thugs but a professional army that had fought the Japanese during World War II. Interestingly, the Viet Minh received funding from the United States, which viewed them as a potent force against a common enemy. When World War II ended, a new war for the independence of Vietnam erupted between the French and the Viet Minh.

The French were ultimately defeated, and the loss of Dien Bien Phu was the straw that broke the French camel's back. The Geneva Accords, which ended France's involvement in Vietnam, called for the temporary partition of the North and South. That division became permanent, creating the nations of North Vietnam and South Vietnam. Sihanouk had to deal with a communist presence in Indochina. He had to be careful in his diplomatic efforts to protect the independence of Cambodia.

---

[i] Osborne, M. (2012, October 18). *The Complex Legacy of Norodom Sihanouk*. Retrieved from Lowryinstitute.org: https://www.lowyinstitute.org/archive/complex-legacy-norodom-sihanouk

Sihanouk's father's death in 1960 permitted him to be made head of state. Cambodia was situated near the hottest point of the Cold War. The Americans were taking a strong interest in South Vietnam as a means of containing communism in Southeast Asia. China saw North Vietnam as an ally that could thwart American ambitions. If Cambodia openly chose sides, it could have harsh consequences for the country. Sihanouk was aware of that dire possibility. Officially, Cambodia would be a neutral country, but at the same time, Sihanouk maneuvered to try to get the best possible deal for Cambodia. His country had endured almost one hundred years of colonial domination, and Sihanouk did not want foreign powers determining its destiny anymore.

Dealing with the West

Indochina was becoming a battleground of the Cold War. Sihanouk wanted military and economic aid from the West, but he did not want Cambodia involved in any proxy war that would further foreign ambitions at Cambodia's expense. His relationships with France were diplomatically correct without permitting the former proprietor of Cambodia to gain any unnecessary influence in the country. However, his dealings with the United States of America required considerable skill.

The United States was adamantly anti-communist and was seeking to thwart any attempts by communism to gain control of countries in Southeast Asia. American involvement in South Vietnam was turning that country into a client state, which was a situation Sihanouk desperately wanted to avoid. He gladly accepted foreign aid from the Americans, but he made it clear that Cambodia's sovereignty was not for sale. America's assistance grew until, in the 1960s, aid from America was approximately 30 percent of Cambodia's defense budget. Americans were also violating Cambodian airspace with military aircraft flying over the country.

Sihanouk's suspicions about America's intentions were heightened when a plot to overthrow him was uncovered in 1959. The leaders included Cambodian officials who were closely connected to the Americans. This and repeated border violations by both the United States and South Vietnam caused Sihanouk to renounce further economic aid in November 1963. He finally broke off diplomatic relations with the United States in 1965.

Collaborating with the Communists

While he was accepting aid from the United States, Sihanouk maintained a close association with China and tried to keep good relations with North Vietnam. His suspicions of the United States caused him to believe that China could serve as a counterbalance to the Americans. It would also serve as a restraint on the Vietnamese. The Chinese believed that being friendly with Cambodia was in their best interests and directed the Cambodian Chinese minority to cooperate with the government and stay out of politics. Cambodia and China signed a treaty of friendship and nonaggression in 1960, cementing a close relationship between the two.

There was a historical lack of trust between North Vietnam and Cambodia. Sihanouk tried to keep relations with North Vietnam stable, and to do this, he took a very risky gamble. The North Vietnamese and the Viet Cong were using eastern Cambodia as a sanctuary area for their soldiers fleeing from American forces. Additionally, part of the supply route into South Vietnam, the Ho Chi Minh Trail, went through parts of Cambodia. Sihanouk was willing to look the other way and permit the communists to use Cambodia as a hiding place, even though this might eventually incur the wrath of the United States.[i]

The Benefits of Neutrality

Cambodia gained some benefits from Sihanouk's efforts to remain neutral. The country received economic aid from both sides of the Cold War. The United States and France gave financial assistance that allowed Cambodia to build up its infrastructure and develop the deepwater port of Sihanoukville (currently known as Kampong Som). Communist China and the Soviet Union also provided financial assistance. The Soviet Union gave scholarships to Cambodian students to help improve their technical expertise.

Sihanouk gained considerable prestige within the nonaligned nations and was seen as an important world figure. However, the game of geopolitics is risky, and the stakes were even higher during the Vietnam War. A military campaign could upset the table and create terrible dangers for Cambodia. Unfortunately, there was a military offensive that

---

[i] Factsanddetails.com. (2014, May). *Cambodia under King Sihanouk*. Retrieved from Factsanddetails.com: https://factsanddetails.com/southeast-asia/Cambodia/sub5_2a/entry-2847.html

radically changed the tide of events in Indochina. It was unexpected and created problems that few people had foreseen.

The Tet Offensive

On January 21st, 1968, the North Vietnamese unleashed an offensive on South Vietnam that shook history. It started out as a diversionary strike against the American military base at Khe Sanh, and on January 30th, the full force of the offensive started. Approximately one hundred South Vietnamese cities and towns were attacked.

The communists' hope that the offensive would create a popular uprising did not materialize. However, the fighting was brutal and lasted for weeks. Intense combat took place in the capital city of Saigon and the old imperial capital of Hue. Ultimately, the United States won a military victory but suffered another type of loss.

The Tet Offensive was a shock. The American public had been led to believe that the United States was winning the Vietnam War and that it would just be a matter of time before the conflict ended. The offensive proved that the Viet Cong (North Vietnamese) were nowhere near being defeated and were a very potent military force. The anti-war movement in the United States intensified, with many people wanting to find a way to get out of the war, even if it meant accepting defeat.[i]

The communist attacks began primarily in South Vietnam. However, sanctuaries in Cambodia were staging grounds for the Tet Offensive, and supplies had come down the Ho Chi Minh Trail through Cambodia. A part of eastern Cambodia known as Parrot's Beak was located a few miles from Saigon, and it was used as a base of operations for the offensive.

The neutrality that Cambodia tried to maintain had been dangerously compromised. The United States began to look seriously at ways to eliminate the military threat coming from Cambodia's eastern frontier, which could include crossing the Cambodian border. Sihanouk continued to insist that Cambodia was neutral, but it was obvious that Cambodian territory was being used in the war. This did not sit well with many Cambodian nationalists. It was bad enough that there were foreign troops in Cambodia. What made things worse was that those soldiers were Vietnamese, a traditional enemy of the Khmers. The chess game

---

[i] Rosenberg, J. (2018, August 17). *Tet Offensive*. Retrieved from ThoughtCo.: https://www.thoughtco.com/tet-offensive-vietnam-1779378

Sihanouk had played for so many years was coming undone, with the pieces scattered all over the board.

The New American Attitude

On January 20th, 1969, Richard Nixon was sworn in as the president of the United States. The Nixon administration's attitude toward Cambodia was not as benign as that of the previous presidency. It was obvious that eastern Cambodia was part of the communist strategy to win in South Vietnam. Cambodia's neutrality was considered a façade, and the United States had to do something about it. Operation Menu was the first response.

Operation Menu was a covert bombing campaign that was carried out from March 18th, 1969, to May 26th, 1970. Base areas and sanctuaries of the North Vietnamese and the Viet Cong were the targets, and the objective was to destroy the enemy's operational capacity. The bombing was intended to be a secret, so information about Operation Menu was kept from the US Congress. B-52 bombers dropped tons of bombs on targets within Cambodia. Historians have argued about the overall success of Operation Menu, but it was clear that the bombing did not end communist military activity. It actually might have indirectly helped bring about another historical event.

A Palace Coup

Lon Nol was a Cambodian general and a critic of the Sihanouk government. He was upset with the presence of North Vietnamese and Viet Cong troops in Cambodia and believed that these foreign soldiers had no business being in the country. He was also skeptical of how the economy was being handled. Another problem that the general had with Sihanouk was the authoritarian style of rule practiced by the head of state.

He was not alone in his negative assessment. Others in the Cambodian government believed that Cambodia had been forced to take a side in the Vietnam War. They hoped that Cambodia would receive needed economic and military support by aligning with the United States. There was a growing belief that Norodom Sihanouk's days as the country's political leader were over. The man had to go.

In March 1970, Sihanouk was on an international tour to gain support from communist countries and promote Cambodia's neutrality when the curtain fell on his days of power. Lon Nol, then Cambodia's prime minister, and the deputy prime minister, Prince Sisowath Sirik

Matak, convinced the Cambodian National Assembly to depose Sihanouk as the head of state. His inability to maintain national sovereignty was the primary reason for his ouster. Sihanouk sought refuge in China, and his asylum request was granted. In the meantime, Nol and his allies declared the creation of the Khmer Republic and aligned the nation with the United States, formally ending any pretense of neutrality. Although the coup was successful, Sihanouk did not accept the results. The country was moving into a civil war.

Chapter 5 - The Khmer Republic and Civil Unrest

It was obvious that Cambodia was now a pawn in the Vietnam War. It was a supply route for the North Vietnamese via the Ho Chi Minh Trail, and the Americans wanted the communist sanctuaries and the supply routes shut down. Sihanouk had tried to play one side off against the other, but that strategy was falling apart. That he was allowing the North Vietnamese to use Cambodia as an operational base infuriated members of the political elite and the military. It was a compromise of Cambodia's sovereignty in their eyes. Something drastic was necessary to correct the nation's course.

The Coup That Ousted Sihanouk

It could be seen as a patriotic act. The conspirators were trying to rid Cambodia of foreigners who could not be trusted. The Khmer Republic was formally announced on October 9th, 1970. The new republic's president was the coup's leader, Lon Nol. The new government switched from being neutral to aligning itself with the United States and South Vietnam. The coup was bloodless, but the aftermath proved to be chaotic and bloody for a number of reasons.

The new president had authoritarian tendencies and was not as charismatic as Sihanouk. Lon Nol sought to mobilize the country to get rid of the North Vietnamese and the Viet Cong. The small Cambodian army was dramatically enlarged as the government tried to use anti-Vietnam sentiments as a means of enlisting troops. The Khmer Republic depended on the United States to provide substantial military and economic aid. Corruption, morale problems, and general inefficiency made it difficult for the military to combat a better-disciplined enemy effectively.

A photograph of Lon Nol.⁷

The Great Divide

Politics was not what divided the Cambodian people. A deep and broad social division existed in the country, and it was the urban population versus rural residents. The upper class included society's elites—government officials, religious leaders, and the military command. The Khmer Republic had done away with royal noble titles and emphasized achievement over heredity, but that did not mean there were no longer distinctions between the upper class and the commoners.

Deferential language was still used when addressing former nobles, and certain behaviors between the aristocracy and the commoners still showed a preference for the former.

There was a middle class in the cities that included teachers, physicians, and shopkeepers. Urban areas were also commercial hubs and places for civil administration, and there was better access to education.

Most Cambodians lived in the countryside and were farmers. Rural inhabitants were isolated from the urban classes, and there was hardly any interaction between the two. Traditional values were important in the farm country, and Buddhism was a significant part of society. The opportunity to have education was limited in the farming areas of Cambodia, and the rural population resented being marginalized by an urban elite.

There was one common trait among the rural people that the Khmer Republic's leaders did not fully appreciate. Despite all of his faults, Norodom Sihanouk was revered by the common people due to his traditional authority and the patronage favors he bestowed. Although the urban upper class did not like him, people in the countryside believed that Sihanouk's ouster was an act of betrayal by the social elite. This perception was going to cause serious challenges for the Khmer Republic government.

Sihanouk's Plan

It would be a mistake to think that Sihanouk ended his days in a debauched lifestyle in Switzerland or Monaco. He had been at the center of power in Cambodia for thirty years and wanted to return to that position. The former head of state was not going to settle for anything less. Sihanouk was willing to engage with anyone who would facilitate his return to power.

He went into exile and was welcomed by the Chinese in Beijing. There, he was provided with considerable support and a safe haven. The Chinese viewed the former Cambodian head of state as an ally who might help them in their geopolitical strategy for Southeast Asia. Sihanouk might be used as a counter to American influence. When Sihanouk traveled to gather support against the Khmer Republic, China gladly helped him.

This cooperation did not mean that Sihanouk was a communist. If anything, he was a Cambodian nationalist. The communist government in China was willing to help him, so the relationship was strategic on both sides. The Chinese wanted to check American progress in Southeast Asia, and Sihanouk wanted to return to power. If the Chinese were willing to help him establish a government in exile, he would accept their assistance.

Sihanouk established the Government of the National Union of Kampuchea (GRONK). It would be the rival of the Khmer Republic and offer resistance to the Lon Nol government. One of the principal groups to be included in the government in exile was the Khmer Rouge.[i]

The Khmer Rouge

Who exactly were the Khmer Rouge?

The Khmer Rouge was a shadowy communist group that was formed in the years after World War II. They were initially influenced by the Communist Party of Vietnam but broke away to pursue a revolution in Cambodia. These were not garden-variety communists, however. They adhered to a rigorous form of Maoism that argued for a classless society based on extreme principles. Agricultural collectivization was necessary, but the Khmer Rouge also wanted to abolish money-based economies and create a pure form of egalitarianism.

They were suspicious of any foreign influence on Cambodian society. What the Khmer Rouge wanted was a form of autarky whereby Cambodia would be completely self-sufficient. To them, this could only be done through a rigorous form of agricultural collectivism and a social transformation without any outside help. Party members characterized their intentions as a "Super Great Leap Forward" in a nod to the Great Leap Forward initiative that China experienced under Mao Zedong in the 1950s. The Khmer Rouge were ardent nationalists. A model for their ideology was the mountain tribes of Cambodia, who practiced a high level of self-sufficiency.

An important feature of the Khmer Rouge doctrine was anti-intellectualism. The Khmer Rouge considered educated people a threat to the agrarian utopia they wished to create in Cambodia. They looked at the educated class and urban dwellers as enemies.

The Khmer Rouge were initially a political organization, but they

---

[i] CENGAGE. (2018, June 27). *Sihanoul, Norodom*. Retrieved from Encyclopedia.com: https://www.encyclopedia.com/people/history/southeast-asia-history-biographies/norodom-sihanouk

moved into an insurgency in 1968 and began actively seeking to take over the Cambodian government.

Sihanouk (third from the left) meeting Mao Zedong in 1965.⁸

Sihanouk and the Khmer Rouge

The relationship between Sihanouk and the Khmer Rouge appears odd at first glance. They had been bitter enemies a few years earlier. Sihanouk even worked to suppress the Khmer Rouge. The best way to describe the eventual alliance was a marriage of convenience. Sihanouk needed a military force to overthrow the Khmer Republic, and the Khmer Rouge needed Sihanouk's popularity with the peasants to recruit members. The former head of state believed that he could manage the Khmer Rouge and that they would help him return to power. This was a serious miscalculation.

The Khmer Rouge had no intention of sharing power with anybody. If Sihanouk had tried to understand the ideology of the Khmer Rouge, he would have been shocked. What the Khmer Rouge had in mind was a complete transformation of Cambodian society in which all the old institutions, including the monarchy, would be abolished. Sihanouk was making a deal with the devil, although he did not appreciate that when he entered into an association with the Khmer Rouge. There was no way that this group of fanatic Maoists ever thought of him as a partner; he was a means by which they would achieve their ends.

Sihanouk played his role as the voice of the Khmer Rouge, urging Cambodians to resist the Khmer Republic and seeking support from international groups. The Khmer Republic became engulfed in a civil war that pitted it against the Khmer Rouge and their North Vietnamese allies. It would have been difficult to survive in the best of times. The country had already been plunged into the worst of times.

Lon Nol started out as the prime minister of the Khmer Republic and then became its president. While the country had the veneer of a functioning republic, it was a military dictatorship in reality. Lon Nol suffered a stroke in 1971, which hampered his ability to be a capable administrator. He was prone to relying on the advice of sycophants and relatives. These advisors were not of much help, as the problems began to increase. Lon Nol became increasingly more autocratic. He made himself marshal in April 1971 and suspended the National Assembly in October. The government was becoming increasingly more corrupt and less able to adequately manage its affairs.

Lon Nol's deficiencies did not go unnoticed. The United States Embassy in Cambodia made a brutal assessment of his competency. The American diplomats did not view Nol as a strong leader. They believed he was not well organized and did not have the love of the people. The Americans felt that he was not somebody who would ordinarily be chosen to lead a modern state; they believed he had become the leader of Cambodia by accident. While the man was a hard worker, his weaknesses were undermining his ability to govern. The assessment of the embassy was that they were stuck with Lon Nol because there was no one else to provide the necessary leadership.[i]

Americans in Cambodia

The American government was propping up the Khmer Republic, which would have collapsed without its support. The United States gave substantial aid to the Khmer Republic, providing hundreds of millions of dollars in military and economic aid to the Cambodian government. The size of the Khmer National Armed Forces (FANK) jumped from approximately 35,000 soldiers in March 1970 to over 200,000 by

---

[i] Office of the Historian. (1974, August 14). *137. Telegram from the Embassy in Cambodia to the Department of State.* Retrieved from History.state.gov:
https://history.state.gov/historicaldocuments/frus1969-76v10/d137

January 1971. This rapid increase would have been impossible without American financial assistance.[i]

Bombing campaigns using B-52 bombers were substantial American contributions to the Khmer Republic's military operations. It is estimated that from March 1969 to August 1973, more than 500,000 tons of ordnance were dropped on over 100,000 sites in Cambodia. FANK was not any closer to a victory because of this, though.[ii]

The Hearts and Minds

The extensive American bombing campaign resulted in multiple civilian deaths. It also led to considerable discontent and resentment among the rural population, and the Khmer Rouge capitalized on that to recruit new soldiers. The inability of FANK to mount successful offensives or hold onto territory enabled the Khmer Rouge to gradually control greater portions of Cambodia. The Khmer Republic was barely holding on. This was when a dramatic turn of events happened that would dramatically alter Cambodian history.

The Beginning of the End

The United States was heavily invested in the Khmer Republic. The Americans had flown in numerous bombing campaigns over Cambodia to neutralize the Ho Chi Minh Trail and clear out any communist sanctuaries in Cambodia. The bombing runs began to target Khmer Rouge military positions, but this did not help at all. Instead, these new bombings caused the destruction of civilian areas and deepened the resentment of the Cambodian farmers. The bombings actually helped the Khmer Rouge's recruiting efforts.

The United States granted considerable military aid to the Khmer Republic in addition to considerable economic assistance. It is estimated that, overall, the Americans gave Cambodia more than $1.6 billion; $1.18 billion was spent on military assistance, and $503 million was spent on economic assistance. The aid did not include the $7 billion the Americans had to expend on bombing campaigns.[iii]

---

[i] Lee, C. J. (2019). *Insurgency: The Cambodian Civil War 1970-1975.* Retrieved from School of Advanced Military Studies: https://apps.dtic.mil/sti/pdfs/AD1083537.pdf

[ii] Lee, C. J. (2019). *Insurgency: The Cambodian Civil War 1970-1975.* Retrieved from School of Advanced Military Studies: https://apps.dtic.mil/sti/pdfs/AD1083537.pdf

[iii] Lee, C. J. (2019). *Insurgency: The Cambodian Civil War 1970-1975.* Retrieved from School of Advanced Military Studies: https://apps.dtic.mil/sti/pdfs/AD1083537.pdf

The American largess did not obtain the intended results. Corruption was rampant in the Khmer Republic, and financial aid often ended up in the hands of government officials and members of the social elite. The peasants received very few benefits.

The Khmer Republic was deeply reliant on American aid. Anything that would affect the money being sent could have dire consequences.

Sihanouk's Role

The Royal Government of National Union of Kampuchea (GRUNK) was a coalition of anti-Lon Nol groups and the Khmer Rouge. The former head of state was the symbolic head. The Khmer Republic had underestimated Sihanouk's popularity among the farmers in rural Cambodia. He was a powerful force to be reckoned with and gave radio broadcasts from exile to encourage the common people to side with the Khmer Rouge. His support of the Khmer Rouge was instrumental in their ultimate success. In a Reuters article published in 2009, Kaing Guek Eav, the commandant of the Khmer Rouge S-21 Tuol Sleng prison camp, conceded that without the active support of Norodom Sihanouk, the Khmer Rouge would not have been successful[i]

Lon Nol's physical condition made it hard for him to be a competent head of state. The stroke he suffered may have taken as much as 20 percent of his intellectual abilities, and he was being influenced by military officers who pocketed the money coming from the United States. Their corruption resulted in Khmer Republic soldiers receiving poor equipment, unreliable pay, and not enough food.

Losing American Support

The American public was getting tired of the role the United States was playing in Southeast Asia. The Vietnam War was losing popular support, which affected relations with the Khmer Republic. In 1970, amid growing concerns about US military expansion in Southeast Asia, Senators John Sherman Cooper and Frank Church introduced an amendment to the Foreign Military Sales Act to prohibit funding for US ground troops and military advisors in Cambodia after July 1st, 1970. Despite this legislative push, President Nixon, on November 18th, 1970, requested congressional approval for $155 million in military aid for the Khmer Republic, prompting further bipartisan resistance.

---

[i] Lee, C. J. (2019). *Insurgency: The Cambodian Civil War 1970-1975*. Retrieved from School of Advanced Military Studies: https://apps.dtic.mil/sti/pdfs/AD1083537.pdf

A revised Cooper-Church Amendment, with tighter provisions, finally passed both chambers on December 22nd, 1970, and became law on January 5th, 1971, firmly restricting further US military involvement in Cambodia.[i]

Battlefield Successes

The Khmer Rouge steadily gained ground. Initially, most of the fighting had been done by the North Vietnamese, but by the end of 1972, the North Vietnamese troops had left Cambodia, leaving the Khmer Rouge responsible for the fighting. They received aid from China, while the North Vietnamese were getting supplies from the Soviet Union.

The Khmer Rouge had a strong base in many of the rural areas of Cambodia, and the government of the Khmer Republic was restricted to the urban centers in the country. The success of the Khmer Rouge was so significant that by early 1973, nearly 85 percent of Cambodia was in the hands of these rebels. The FANK could not mount an offensive.[ii]

The Loss of American Assistance

It was clear that the Khmer Republic was not able to resist the Khmer Rouge and their allies. The American government was becoming inclined to cut its losses and leave Cambodia to its fate. On January 27th, 1973, the Paris Peace Accords were signed. The United States began to withdraw its military forces from Vietnam. However, bombing campaigns continued in Cambodia until August of that year.

Financial aid continued, but it was severely reduced. The Case-Church Amendment was passed in June 1973 and prohibited military activity in Cambodia without congressional approval. The US bombing of Cambodia ended on August 16th, 1973. The Khmer Republic was now on its own.[iii]

---

[i] Glass, A. (2015, November 18). *Nixon Asks Congress to Fund Aid for Cambodia, Nov. 18, 1970*. Retrieved from Politico.com: https://www.politico.com/story/2015/11/nixon-asks-congress-to-fund-aid-for-cambodia-nov-18-1970-215912

[ii] Cambodiatribunal.org. (2024, December 16). *Khmer Rouge History*. Retrieved from Cambodiatribunal.org: https://cambodiatribunal.org/history/cambodian-history/khmer-rouge-history/

[iii] Archives.gov. (2024, December 15). *Episode 9: Crossing into Cambodia*. Retrieved from Archives.gov: https://www.archives.gov/exhibits/remembering-vietnam-online-exhibit-episodes-9-12

Final Victory

The Khmer Republic's resistance was crumbling. By 1975, the republic had only Phnom Penh and a few towns along the Mekong to its name. The Khmer Rouge began their final assault in January 1975. They cut off the Mekong supply route and began to move toward Phnom Penh. They were able to surround the capital, and on April 1st, 1975, Lon Nol resigned. The Americans executed Operation Eagle Pull on April 12th, 1975, and evacuated US nationals. The Khmer Rouge entered the city of Phnom Penh on April 17th, 1975. The Cambodian Civil War was over. The Khmer Rouge had won.

It is enticing to wonder what was going through Norodom Sihanouk's mind when Phnom Penh fell. He made a career out of being a very cagey politician and having a sense of which way the wind was blowing. Now, the Khmer Rouge were the winners, and they had Sihanouk to thank for generating the popular support that eased the way to victory. Did Sihanouk believe that the Khmer Rouge would recognize their debt to him? After all, he had suppressed the Khmer Rouge in earlier years, and the alliance was one that was mutually advantageous. The victory might have clouded his political senses, and he might have thought that a peaceful period of cooperation and coexistence was about to begin. The master politician was going to be grievously mistaken.

Chapter 6 - The Khmer Rouge Era: Democratic Kampuchea's Tragedy

The Cambodians could give a collective sigh of relief. The war that had torn the country apart for five years was over. There would be no more bombing runs over the rice fields. The foreigners were gone, and Cambodia was now able to decide its destiny. The citizens believed they would be able to enjoy the benefits of peace and quiet. They were horribly mistaken.

The Justice of the Victors

The people of Phnom Penh barely had time to catch their breath when they found out firsthand who their new rulers were and what their intentions were. A few days after the final occupation of Phnom Penh, the Khmer Rouge ordered the evacuation of the city. All the inhabitants were going to be sent to the country. They deceived the inhabitants by telling them they would only be moving a few miles outside of the city and would be allowed to return in a couple of days. Of course, the victors had other plans for all of these people. Residents were forced out of their homes at gunpoint. Up to two million city dwellers were marched out of the capital. The same thing happened in other Cambodian cities.

While the population was moving, the Khmer Rouge executed as many civil servants, police, and military officers of the former Khmer Republic as they could get their hands on. A bizarre form of tyranny began to settle in the war-devastated country.

The Rationale of the Khmer Rouge

The Khmer Rouge was motivated by a radical form of Marxism-Leninism. It is important to explore their belief system a little bit deeper to understand the horror of what the Khmer Rouge was going to do to Cambodia and what they did in the years that followed their victory.

The Khmer Rouge believed in a Maoist interpretation of the standard communist text. They thought the peasant class was the foundation of any successful revolution and that the goal of a purified society would only be achieved if Cambodia were an agricultural economy based in the countryside. The society that they envisioned would be an authoritarian dictatorship where no dissent was allowed. Existing societal norms and practices were going to be broken down and replaced with the new order. Appropriately, they referred to 1975 as Year Zero, the start of the rejuvenation of Cambodia and the beginning of its new history.

Urban areas were seen as evil places. The Khmer Rouge believed that cities such as Phnom Penh were bastions of Western corruption. Moreover, they believed that cities encouraged foreign dependency, exploitative capitalism, and jaded morals. The people needed to be taken out of these dens of iniquity and brought into the countryside, where they could be reeducated and turned into devoted followers of the revolution. The best way to accomplish all of their objectives was to isolate Cambodia from the evil influences of the outside world, even if that meant a complete disruption of daily lives.

The Terror Begins

It was going to be a complete makeover of Cambodian society. All forms of temptation and capitalist influences were to be destroyed. The Khmer Rouge did the following in order to begin the process of rejuvenation.

- They abolished money.
- Public schools, pagodas, mosques, churches, universities, government buildings, and shops were closed.
- Private property, non-revolutionary entertainment, and public and private transportation were abolished.
- All Cambodian citizens were deprived of basic rights. If three or more people gathered to chat with each other, they were considered enemies and were subject to arrest and even execution. Everyone was expected to wear black costumes, which were the revolutionary clothing of the Khmer Rouge.

An example of Khmer Rouge clothing.⁹

Revenge as Motivation

Most people today (and even then) will gasp in disbelief at the savagery and cruelty the Khmer Rouge showed to their fellow Cambodian citizens. It was more than just ideology, though. The Khmer Rouge had a deep hatred for intellectuals and city dwellers. They blamed the urban elite for the problems that Cambodia had suffered, and many Khmer Rouge families had been the victims of the bombing campaigns. Taking revenge on the urban population was justifiable in their eyes. People who lived in the cities were corrupt, evil, and debased. Only through a strict regimen of purification could these urban dwellers eventually become productive citizens of the new state. Consequently, their sins would be purged through the fire of what the Khmer Rouge decided was going to happen.

The Master of Cambodia's Disaster

There was an evil genius behind the Khmer Rouge. He was the primary source of the blueprint designed to transform Cambodia into a radically egalitarian society. His name was Pol Pot.

He was born with the name Saloth Sar on May 19th, 1925, into a wealthy family. There was nothing extraordinary about his life until he received a scholarship in 1949 to go to Paris to study radio technology. Paris was then a place of residence for Cambodian intellectuals, especially those who had leftist views. Pol Pot was exposed to communist ideology while he was a student, and it would transform his life.

Pol Pot joined the French Communist Party and began to read the works of Vladimir Lenin and Karl Marx. Pol Pot was a Cambodian nationalist who wanted independence for his country and to have it be liberated from Western colonialism. Marxist-Leninism seemed to be the best way to change Cambodia for the better.

Another communist theorist was going to have a dominant influence on the young student's thoughts: Mao Zedong. Classical Marxist-Leninism celebrates the worker who is from a manufacturing setting. Mao took a different stance. He stressed the significance of the peasantry and their role in any social revolution. To Mao, the farmers were a primary part of the Cambodian workforce, and Pol Pot saw the logic of addressing the needs of the peasants as opposed to factory workers.

Pol Pot returned to Cambodia in January 1953 and became part of the Khmer People's Revolutionary Party (KPRP). His day job was as a teacher at a private school, but at night, he worked with others to plan a revolution. He assisted in reorganizing the KPRP so that it would be more in line with the theories of Marxist-Leninism. Government suppression forced him and others to find refuge in northern Cambodia. He eventually became the head of the party and, with the newly formed Khmer Rouge guerrilla army, started a national uprising in 1968. Although the Khmer Rouge was able to gain some territory in the northeast, the revolution did not pick up any steam, and there was little popular support. That all changed with the 1970 coup.

Pol Pot envisioned a complete makeover of Cambodian society. There would be no private property, and there would be a classless society. Cambodia would be self-sufficient and beholden to no foreign power. There was a sinister side to his intentions, though. Pol Pot hated the intellectuals and professionals. He considered these people to be corrupt and a bad influence on society. He wanted them gone, and that meant killing them. He also wanted total control of society, which included personal relationships between people. Pol Pot's idea of efficiency was to kill anybody who stood in his way. He had the ability to ruthlessly do that when the Khmer Rouge came to power.

Into the Fields

The Khmer Rouge initially told the residents of Phnom Penh they needed to be evacuated to avoid American bombing. It was a strategic lie used to move these urban dwellers into the country with as little resistance as possible from them. People evacuated Phnom Penh carrying very few possessions with them. Soon, the roads leading out of the city were crowded with evacuees, and only a few were offered transportation. The rest walked. Food was not readily available, although there were tons of provisions in the storehouses in Kampong Som.

The forced march was a human tragedy. Children lost their parents, and others could not find their relatives. The Khmer Rouge did not hesitate to shoot anyone who resisted orders. It was not long before the roads were cluttered with corpses. The people were forced to march in the hot sun with little food or water. It is estimated that twenty thousand people died during the evacuation alone. When Pol Pot entered Phnom Penh on April 23rd, 1975, he was walking in a ghost town that once held well over a million people.

The New Order

The Khmer Rouge wanted Cambodia to be a blank slate. This meant murdering anyone whom they suspected might be a potential troublemaker. They killed as many former government workers and Khmer Republic soldiers as they could find. They expanded the execution list to include people with an education. Entire villages were even massacred by them.

The barbarity seemed gratuitous and extreme. Moving the population to the countryside included forcing twenty-five thousand patients to leave their hospital beds in Phnom Penh and being marched into the fields. When it became apparent that the Khmer Rouge would kill anyone for no reason at all, Cambodians started to flee for their lives. In the first year, approximately twenty thousand Cambodians sought refuge in

Thailand. The stories they told about what was happening in Cambodia were chilling.

Year Zero was more than a political slogan for the Khmer Rouge. They wanted Cambodian society to return to its roots in the rice fields, which the Khmer Rouge saw as a means of purifying the people. Cambodians would perform agricultural labor even if they had never lived on a farm before. They would work on collectivized farms and be required to perform hard manual labor under the hot sun.

The Khmer Rouge set an economic goal of self-sufficiency. Cambodia would be free from any foreign dependence, be able to feed the population, and create surpluses for exports. It is understandable, in a way, why this goal was set. Cambodia had relied on foreign assistance for years, and it had turned the country into a client state that was dependent on others. Self-sufficiency would give the Cambodians economic freedom, and it would also gain respect for the new government. A Four-Year Plan was announced in 1976, and it stressed the cultivation of rice. The annual yield was expected to be three tons of rice per hectare (approximately 2.5 acres). Furthermore, the country was expected to achieve two rice harvests per year.

These were ambitious goals, and the people were expected to achieve them. It would be difficult, if not impossible, to meet those figures. Cambodia had been destroyed by years of war. The number of draft animals, such as oxen, that were traditionally used to plow the fields had been drastically reduced because of the aerial bombings. The job of creating grain surpluses was the responsibility of "new people" who had been forcibly relocated from the urban areas. They did not have the skillset to be effective farmers, but this did not make a difference to the Khmer Rouge. This new workforce was expected to deliver results. Anything less than maximum effort was not going to be tolerated, and those who appeared to be slackers were going to be brutally punished. The country was being turned into a massive slave labor camp.

Dark Days Set In

The official name for Cambodia was changed to Democratic Kampuchea on January 5th, 1976, and the country wrote a new constitution. "Democratic" was not the right word for this government because the Khmer Rouge was in charge of everything. Any form of opposition was ruthlessly suppressed. Cambodians were forced to work long hours in the rice fields and were not fed adequately. The hard work and patriotic slogans were no substitute for efficient management. The Khmer Rouge were excellent guerrilla fighters, but they were terrible managers. Agricultural products suffered from unrealistic goals and incompetent supervisors. There were shortages of all types. There was a serious deficiency in medical supplies and attention. There were acute shortages of necessary drugs, and the Khmer Rouge had killed off many of the doctors, assuming them to be degenerate intellectuals. Disease and exhaustion took a deadly toll as workers dropped dead in the fields.

The ambitious goals for rice production were not met. Instead of blaming incompetent managers, however, the Khmer Rouge automatically assumed that the farm workers were lazy or that there were enemies of the state in the rice paddies hoping to destroy the revolution. Consequently, the Khmer Rouge pushed the people harder.

The already scanty rations were cut, and farm workers only received a few ounces of rice with which to feed their families. Those who dared to go into the wilderness to forage for food ended up in interrogation centers or murdered on the spot whenever they were caught.

Individuals were nothing more than cogs in the wheel of revolutionary progress. They worked until they were physically no longer able to, and then they were eliminated. The Khmer Rouge did not pity anybody; educated people were simply useless eaters in their minds.

The government did not target only educated people. Ethnic and religious minorities were also in its crosshairs. The Vietnamese were hated and suspected of being invaders. There was a small Muslim community in Cambodia whose people had lived there for generations. They were smeared with pig blood and then killed with farm implements.

The Senseless Slaughter

The accounts of what the Khmer Rouge did to the farm workers seem pathological. The techniques used would fit nicely into a horror movie, but none of them were fiction. The testimonies and recollections of the survivors bear witness to the horror they faced.

Any farm worker who was unable to meet production quotas or disobeyed orders was considered

a counterrevolutionary, and they would be subject to various punishments. Starvation was one of the milder ones. The Khmer Rouge beat people with farm tools, waterboarded them, and/or amputated body parts. These were not just used for punishment but also to coerce victims into signing false confessions or spying on other people.

The situation was made worse by the Khmer Rouge guards. They ate well while they watched half-starved people work. Some of the guards had a very obvious sadistic streak. They would often throw leftover food out on the field and laugh as people scrambled to get the half-eaten morsels.

The Notorious Prison System

Pol Pot was Brother Number One to the Khmer Rouge, and anyone who criticized or resisted him was thought of as an enemy of the state. The governing regime was called Angkar ("organization"), and loyalty was expected to be unquestioned. The Khmer Rouge had no problem in arresting anyone, even if it was not justified. Their attitude was summed up in one of their slogans, "It is better to arrest ten people by mistake than to let one guilty person go free."

Problems meeting production goals made the Khmer Rouge suspect that deliberate sabotage was being practiced, and the culprits had to be rooted out and severely punished. Those who were not fully dedicated to the success of Angkar had to be purified. To accomplish this enforced cleansing, an enormous security apparatus that included almost two hundred prisons was established. These were places where the inmates would be questioned, tortured, and, if necessary, executed.

The worst place of incarceration was known officially as S-21, but it is now better known as Tuol Sleng. During the time that it was used as a prison, between fourteen thousand and seventeen thousand Cambodians were imprisoned there. It is reported that only twelve of those people survived. The prison's population was not only ordinary Cambodians but also Vietnamese and Muslims. Tuol Sleng was full of prisoners who were taken from the ranks of the Khmer Rouge.

Jacques Mallet du Pan, a royalist writer during the French Revolution, is credited with stating that revolutions will devour their own children. That phenomenon was happening in Cambodia, as the Khmer Rouge began to turn on each other. The leadership was becoming paranoid because of the massive failures, and members of the Khmer Rouge were being suspected of working for the CIA or Vietnam. The government began rounding up those who were suspected of treason, and it was not limited to just the individual; families and subordinates were also liable for arrest and elimination. The revolution was beginning to get out of control, and torture techniques, such as electric shock, indiscriminate beatings, and waterboarding, were used at Tuol Sang to extract confessions. It did not matter if the victim had actually committed a crime or not.

International Reaction

Mass executions were becoming common, and the places where these took place were also the burial grounds. These mass graves became known as the killing fields. The most notorious one was at Choeung Ek, where nearly seventeen thousand remains of victims have been found. The final number of people murdered by the Khmer Rouge from 1975 to 1979 is estimated to be between 1.5 million and 3 million.

Democratic Kampuchea was a closed country, and the international community was not fully aware of what was going on. However, refugees found ways to cross the border into Thailand and Vietnam. Aid workers at refugee camps along the Thai border began to hear the stories of forced labor and executions. These tales of horror were shared with the outside world. The initial reactions were shock and outrage. The United Nations provided immense human relief aid, and in April 1978, United States President Jimmy Carter publicly condemned the Khmer Rouge.

Unfortunately, nothing was done to stop the genocide. The United States was through with Southeast Asia, and sending an expeditionary force to liberate the Cambodian people was out of the question. The Khmer Rouge denied any report of atrocity and continued to murder innocent people. The killing fields were active until 1979.

The 20th century has witnessed horrible human disasters, including the Armenian genocide, the Holodomor, and the Holocaust. The Cambodian killing fields are consistent with the brutality and inhumanity of these mass slaughters. Roughly one-fourth of Cambodia's population at the time was murdered by the Khmer Rouge. This does not include the thousands that were killed in the aerial bombing and fighting that took place from 1970 to 1975. The destruction was grim, and it is important to assess the damage that was done.

An Economic Disaster

Pol Pot's idea for Cambodia was for it to be completely self-sufficient and no longer dependent on any foreign aid whatsoever. This meant that a nation already damaged by earlier military action would have to find a way to rebuild and be productive. The goals that were set by the Khmer Rouge would be difficult even for a nation with a healthy economy.

The perfect society that the Khmer Rouge envisioned would be one where there was no private property, commercial markets, or even a currency with which to conduct financial transactions. However, these are the basics for any healthy economy, and what the Khmer Rouge wanted in its place was an agrarian society without any class distinctions. This dream did not consider the wretched condition of the Cambodian economy. Banks were among the first casualties of the new economic order.

The people were forced onto collective farms and had to give up other private property. The lessons of the Ukrainian Holodomor detail what happens when people are forced to become part of collective farms. A troubling problem with collectivization is that urban people are required to do hard physical labor in the fields with insufficient nutrition or rest. Because these people have no experience with farming techniques, mistakes are bound to happen.

A healthy economy needs a sound infrastructure as well. This means more than just roads. The Khmer Rouge took an already war-ravaged infrastructure and destroyed it. Schools and hospitals were closed, and the doctors, who were viewed as traitors and intellectuals, were killed. An irrigation system is vital for an agricultural society. The canals and dikes that were built had faulty construction, and the Cambodian irrigation system, which was the pride of the Khmer Empire centuries before, was largely ineffective.

Human capital is necessary for any nation's economy to thrive. The Khmer Rouge killed the intellectuals and skilled professionals, which resulted in a lack of knowledge and cognitive resources required to rebuild a broken economy. The economic transformation that the Khmer Rouge wanted to achieve was more ambitious than in any other communist country. However, rice production quotas were not met, and the people were underfed. The economic dream of Pol Pot was going nowhere.

The Collapse of the Social Structure

The family was an important part of Cambodian society. It was the glue that helped keep the nation whole. The Khmer Rouge wanted a classless society, and family units meant little to them. The evacuation of Phnom Penh and other cities created serious social problems. People were separated from their families, and communities were torn apart. The people did not have any social anchors in this new regime. The problems became even worse due to the banning of religious practices. Those who survived the Khmer Rouge's reign of terror were left with psychological scars and suffered from mental health issues for years.

The collective farms were supposed to provide sufficient food to sustain the population. This did not happen. The daily rations per person in 1977 were 570 grams of rice. Most people would only get between 250 and 500 grams. Children, the sick, and the elderly suffered the most from malnutrition and starvation. Lack of medical supplies meant the workforce was physically weakened by disease.

Ethnic cleansing took place as well. Ethnic and religious minorities, including Chinese, Cham Muslims, and Vietnamese, were targeted. This would impact roughly 20 percent of Cambodia's population because there were twenty minority groups within the country's borders. These people were all enemies of the state in the minds of the Khmer Rouge. It is believed that twenty thousand Cham were killed by the Khmer Rouge.

The Vietnamese were originally to be expelled, but then the plan switched to mass murder. The Khmer Rouge did not respect international borders and crossed into Vietnam, where they killed close to thirty thousand Vietnamese civilians. The worst massacre occurred at Ba Chuc in southern Vietnam. There, over three thousand Vietnamese were killed from April 18th to April 30th, 1978.

Chinese Cambodians were accused of exploiting the Cambodian people and being closely associated with capitalism. There were 425,000 ethnic Chinese in Cambodia in 1975. At the end of 1979, there were only 200,000. The irony is that even though the People's Republic of China knew that ethnic Chinese were being persecuted and killed, it did not protest.

Muslims were not the only religious group targeted for slaughter. Democratic Kampuchea was atheist, so all religions were repressed vigorously. It is reported that nearly fifty thousand Buddhist monks alone were massacred. Analysis of the demographic data estimates that 81 percent of all violent deaths were men. This meant that somewhere between 50 and 70 percent of Cambodia's working-age men were killed by the Khmer Rouge.

Skulls at the Choeung Ek Memorial.[10]

Implements of Death

The Nazis in the Holocaust used firing squads and gas chambers to kill innocent people. Starvation and death from exhaustion were common means of killing people as well, but the Khmer Rouge used other means to dispose of people. They wanted to save bullets, so it was common to kill victims with pickaxes or bamboo sticks. The victims were often made to dig their own graves.

Using gas chambers in Nazi extermination camps provided a degree of anonymity; the executioners saw the dead bodies after they opened the gas chambers and did not watch their victims perish. By using clubs or other blunt instruments, the Khmer Rouge were able to see the anguish in their victims' eyes and hear the screams of the person being killed. It apparently did not seem to matter. After all, these were enemies of the state or useless eaters whose deaths would mean a few less mouths to feed. Systematic torture was used at prison facilities.

The Nightmare of Tuol Sleng

Only a handful of those who were held in the Tuol Sleng prison survived. Living conditions were so squalid that many prisoners died before they could be formally executed. The Khmer Rouge wanted confessions out of people, and they would delay outright killing a person until they had a statement from them. Obtaining that information would include using torture tactics such as pulling out fingernails or suffocating prisoners with plastic bags. Electric shock and rape were standard practices.

Prisoners could include members of the Khmer Rouge. The government became increasingly paranoid and suspected that there were traders among the rank and file of the Khmer Rouge. Consequently, high-ranking officials and soldiers could be found among the prison population. Any suspicion of disloyalty was treated as treason.

There were, of course, other reasons that were more personal. It was not unusual for people to settle a grudge by denouncing a rival, and Khmer Rouge members would accuse their comrades in order to escape being suspected. Career advancement was also a motive. Eliminating a rival or a hated superior could clear the way for a member to rise in the ranks.

The cells in Tuol Sleng.[11]

Children were both victims and executioners. The Khmer Rouge did not hesitate to kill the children of executed men to avoid attempts at revenge. The Khmer Rouge practiced forms of brainwashing to make them obey. Children were encouraged to denounce their parents, and they were conditioned to obey orders without hesitating. Everything was to serve the objective of creating a classless society where everyone would think the same thoughts.

The Fate of Norodom Sihanouk

Norodom Sihanouk was meant to be the nominal head of state for Cambodia. He arrived in Phnom Penh on September 9th, 1975. He walked into a wasteland. In the once bustling city of Phnom Penh, streets and sidewalks that had once been filled with people noisily coming and going, there was only deathly silence. There was nothing that suggested Phnom Penh had been an important capital in Asia a year before. Hundreds of thousands of people had been moved out. There was no precise estimate of how many had been killed or had died in the five months since the fall of the city, but it must have been in the thousands. Sihanouk was justifiably shocked at what he saw.

An overwhelming sense of guilt might have gripped him. The Khmer Rouge was nothing more than another dissident group holding on to some territory in 1969. It was Sihanouk's endorsement that jump-started the Khmer Rouge and helped them gain the recruits and military support required to overthrow the government. These black-shirted fanatics were now in control of Cambodia, and they could ignore Sihanouk if they wanted to do that. Sihanouk gradually realized that he was nothing but a figurehead with no real say in politics. The master of diplomacy and subtle backroom maneuvering had been duped.

He came to understand that even though he was very popular with the public, he was expendable. Whenever the Khmer Rouge decided that he was no longer useful, they would replace him. That day finally came in April 1976. Vice-Premier Khieu Samphan announced in a radio broadcast that Norodom Sihanouk had resigned as the chief of state. The former king of Cambodia would receive a pension, and a statue would be erected in his honor. This was all apparently intended to appease those who had any loyalty remaining for the man. The resignation might not have been voluntary because Sihanouk was placed under house arrest. He was eventually given permission to leave the country for China. He was one of the lucky ones.

The narrative of what happened in the killing fields of Cambodia is still being assessed. There may be more graves yet to be found and bodies dug up. The crime against humanity was terrible, and what it did to Cambodia is beyond normal comprehension.

Chapter 7 - Vietnamese Occupation and the People's Republic of Kampuchea

Communist academics have stressed the solidarity of communism and how nations that have accepted Marxist-Leninist theory are united in a common revolution. That is not true. Rivalries and animosities between two countries are often part of their histories and can go back centuries. This is true with Cambodia and Vietnam. The antagonism between the two nations goes back to the days of the Khmer Empire. The fact that both were communist in the 1970s does not mean the old rivalries and grudges were tossed aside.

The Khmer Rouge persecuted Cambodians who were ethnic Vietnamese. The new regime considered them to be outsiders and possibly traitors. The refugees that flowed across the border into what was the Socialist Republic of Vietnam told their stories of persecution and what was going on inside Democratic Kampuchea. The Vietnamese government was very concerned about what was happening. The two countries were communist, but their ideologies were different. The Khmer Rouge were radical Maoists, and the Cambodian government was closely connected to the People's Republic of China. Vietnam, on the other hand, was governed by a more pragmatic regime that was closely aligned with the Soviet Union.

There is land in Vietnam that historically was Cambodian. The Khmer Rouge wanted to reclaim that territory. They also wanted to capture those Cambodians who had fled the country. The Khmer Rouge began to make military forays into Vietnam, attacking the border villages. These were not minor assaults. In September 1977, the Khmer Rouge launched a major incursion, sending three divisions about six miles into Vietnam's Tay Ninh province and killing over a thousand civilians. Vietnam responded in December 1977 with a counterattack, deploying around thirty thousand troops to repel the invaders. The intention at the time was to force the Khmer Rouge to negotiate. The two sides were not evenly matched.

The Vietnamese had the best army in Southeast Asia, and its battle-tested veterans had waged successful campaigns against the French and Americans. The Vietnamese quickly overpowered what troops the Khmer Rouge had and moved into the Svay Rieng province of Cambodia. Instead of negotiating, the Cambodian government severed diplomatic relations with Vietnam.

The Vietnamese were within twenty-four miles of Phnom Penh on January 6th, 1978, when the Vietnamese government decided to withdraw. They took with them prisoners, civilian refugees, and some very important political leaders.

The leaders of Democratic Kampuchea failed to realize they were dealing with a neighbor with a significant military. Instead, they bragged about having driven the foreigners out. Official propaganda provided some saber-rattling. Attempts at diplomacy, including meetings between Vietnam and Cambodia held in Beijing in early 1978, proved futile. Mediation efforts by China also failed. The two countries were moving closer and closer to a full-scale war.

The Final Straw

Pol Pot wanted eastern Cambodia to be cleansed of any Vietnamese influence and had troops move into that area to eliminate any person suspected of being a traitor. The Cambodian army crossed the border into Vietnam on April 18th, 1978, and the result of the incursion was the Ba Chuc massacre. The Vietnamese were enraged and conducted bombing sorties in June 1978. It was by this time that Vietnam concluded that a regime change in Cambodia was necessary.

The incursions were not the only reasons the Vietnamese felt that way. The government in Hanoi had a genuine humanitarian concern, and something had to be done to stop the ongoing genocide. Another significant reason was the deterioration of relations between China and Vietnam. The Soviet Union and China were rivals in Southeast Asia despite being communist regimes. Vietnam's relationship with the Soviet Union created tension between it and its northern neighbor. It was strategically sensible to neutralize China's close ally, Cambodia.

The propaganda war between the two countries was heating up. Vietnamese newspapers were calling for international intervention in Cambodia, and the government was bringing together a sizeable military task force. On December 25th, 1978, 150,000 Vietnamese troops invaded Democratic Kampuchea. A full-scale war between the two countries now erupted.[i]

The Vietnamese called their offensive a "campaign to defend the border," but there was nothing defensive on the Vietnamese side. Instead, they wanted a regime change in Phnom Penh and the end to the Khmer Rouge threat to the Vietnamese border towns. The opportunity to establish a pro-Vietnamese government was clearly an objective.

The results were short and swift. Cambodia's defenses were overwhelmed, and the coordination of the Vietnamese advance was apparent. Pol Pot's army could not mount an effective resistance against the Vietnamese offensive. The Vietnamese were able to capture Phnom Penh on January 7th, 1979. The war lasted no more than two weeks, and the Khmer leadership was sent running. The speed of the victory must have amazed even the Vietnamese, who no doubt thought that the Khmer Rouge had tight control of the country. There were a number of reasons for the quick collapse.

---

[i] Vietnamtheartofwar.com. (2024, December 18). *25 December 1978: Vietnam Invades Cambodia*. Retrieved from Vietnamtheartofwar.com: https://vietnamtheartofwar.com/1978/12/01/25-december-1978-vietnam-invades-cambodia/.

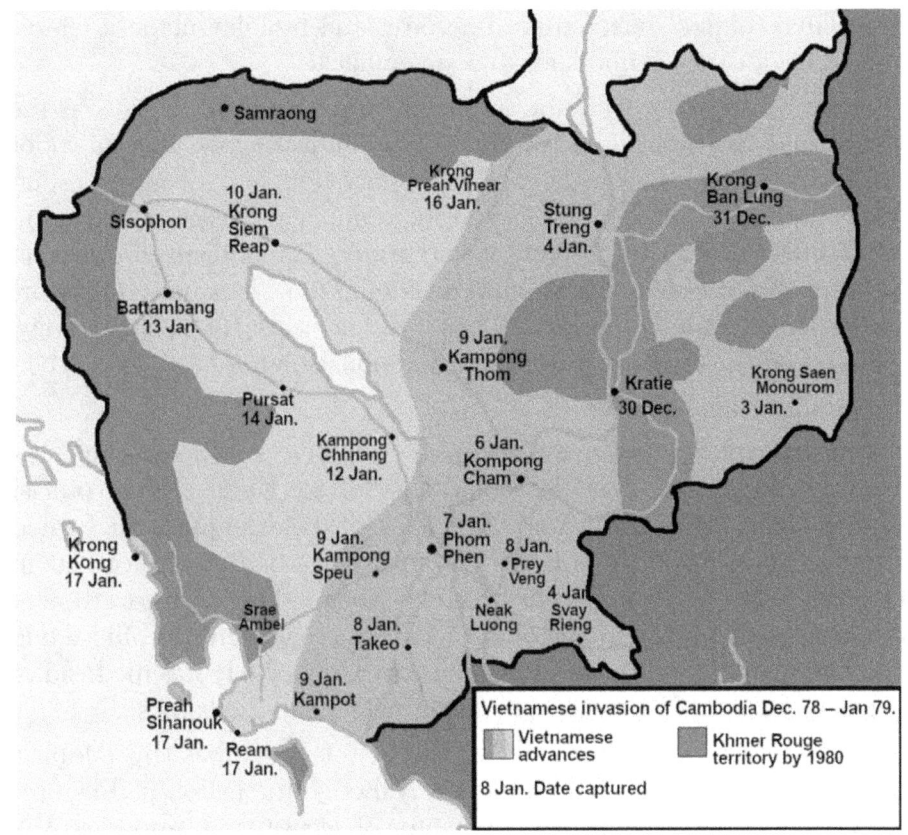

The Vietnamese invasion of Cambodia.[12]

Cambodian propaganda before the war promoted the courage and efficiency of the country's army. The Cambodians had 200,000 men in uniform, which ought to have enabled them to mount a stiff wall against the invaders. However, the image of a capable fighting force was concocted. The National Army of Democratic Kampuchea was no match for what Vietnam had.

Cambodian troops needed to be better trained and needed more modern weapons to defend the country adequately. Moreover, the government was suspicious of its own military and purged the ranks of officers of any who were suspected of being less than enthusiastic about the new regime. Many competent and experienced commanders were imprisoned or executed.

The Khmer Rouge had been victorious as a guerrilla force against a weak and corrupt Khmer Republic Army. On the other hand, the Vietnamese army was a battle-ready force with better tactics and more disciplined soldiers. Vietnamese firepower and mobility made it almost impossible for the Cambodians to counterattack.

A significant reason for the Khmer Rouge's ultimate defeat was the way it had governed the country. The infrastructure was in poor condition, and a combination of semi-starvation and near-exhaustion tactics produced soldiers who lacked the stamina to engage in successful combat. There was no absolute loyalty to the Cambodian government. In fact, many people in Cambodia considered the Vietnamese liberators and welcomed their presence. There was no sense of national unity, even though the invading forces were traditional enemies.

Another Name Change

On January 8th, 1979, the People's Republic of Kampuchea was formally announced. Its leader would be a former Khmer Rouge official named Heng Samrin. He was the leader of the Kampuchean United Front for National Salvation (KUFNS), a resistance group formed in December 1978 to oppose the Khmer Rouge. The new government would be staffed by members of the KUFNS. Heng Samrin's official title was chairman of the People's Revolutionary Council. He was the head of state, and he would be an acceptable puppet for the Vietnamese.[i]

The primary governing body of the new country was the People's Revolutionary Council of Kampuchea. Although the nation had its own army, Vietnam was the primary guarantor of security in Cambodia. Any vestige of Maoism was gone, and the People's Republic of Kampuchea was firmly in the grip of its neighbor. While it was better than having the Khmer Rouge in charge, Cambodia faced a new set of challenges.

Lack of International Recognition

The People's Republic of Kampuchea (PRK) did not get the endorsement of the United Nations. The coalition government of Democratic Kampuchea held the Cambodian seat. In other words, the Khmer Rouge might have been defeated in the field, but in diplomatic circles, it was still thought of as the official Cambodian government. The PRK received scarce international recognition. Chinese opposition to the new government was a major factor.

---

[i] Kimertimeskh.com. (2024, May 24). *Ninety Years in the Life of Samdech Heng Samrin*. Retrieved from Kimertimeskh.com: https://www.khmertimeskh.com/501494144/ninety-years-in-the-life-of-samdech-heng-samrin/

Cold War politics also played a role. Ironically, the United States government did not recognize the PRK but instead recognized the Coalition Government of Democratic Kampuchea (CGDK), which included the Khmer Rouge among its member parties. It is ironic that a democracy such as the United States would recognize a government that included the Khmer Rouge, but the international community essentially isolated the PRK.

The PRK also faced considerable internal opposition that hampered its ability to govern effectively.

The Internal Conflict in Cambodia

The Khmer Rouge was defeated, but it was not eliminated. Its supporters had retreated to the Thai border country and were organizing for a guerrilla war against the PRK. Anti-communist groups also resisted the authority of the PRK, and it appeared that no matter how hard the Cambodians tried, there was not going to be peace in the land. There were too many factions fighting to gain control, and innocent civilians were continually caught in the crossfire.

The resistance to the PRK merged into a group known as the Coalition Government of Democratic Kampuchea. It was comprised of the Khmer Rouge, various political groups, and people who supported the restoration of the monarchy. It may appear strange that people who would ordinarily be against the Khmer Rouge were willing to ally with this Maoist organization that had done so much damage within Cambodia. The reasons for this strange alliance included the PRK being in close association with Vietnam, the traditional enemy of the Cambodians. The PRK was also not doing a good job of rebuilding the economy. There was much to do, and the Khmer Rouge had destroyed a lot of the economic infrastructure, but people believed that the PRK was not doing enough. Their resistance was backed by foreign nations such as the United States and China. Their rationale was to try to curb the power of the Vietnamese in the region.

The Landmines

Both sides used landmines. Although landmines were used earlier in the conflict, they became a defensive weapon of choice in the 1980s. The Khmer Rouge employed landmines to defend their border strongholds. The PRK also used these anti-personnel devices to secure their positions within Cambodia and to inhibit guerrilla raids coming across from Thailand. Supply routes were protected by using landmines.

The best example of landmine use was the K5 mine belt. This was a stretch of land along the Thai-Cambodian border that extended for hundreds of miles and was intended to keep back the Khmer Rouge who were trying to cross the Thai border into Cambodia.[i]

Estimates suggest that four to six million landmines were laid in Cambodia. These could be mine belts, or they could be anti-personnel devices scattered indiscriminately across stretches of land. Thousands of Cambodians were either killed or crippled by the landmines and booby traps that the PRK and the CGDK set.

Cultural Restoration

The Vietnamese were the guarantor of the PRK's security, and the Cambodian government worked to rehabilitate the country despite the military resistance from the opposition. An aggressive campaign to improve the condition of the Cambodian people was set forth in the 1981 Constitution. The Khmer language was recognized as the national language, and the government worked to universalize literacy in Khmer.

The educational system in Cambodia was in a shambles, thanks to the Khmer Rouge, and the PRK expended time, capital, and efforts to restore the educational system of the country. This was not easy since most of the teachers had been killed by the Khmer Rouge. However, in a few years, primary school enrollment was back at levels not seen since 1969. The literacy rates of Cambodians gradually increased. Vocational training efforts were initiated to give people the technical skills necessary to enhance economic development.[ii]

Religion was an important part of Cambodian life before the Khmer Rouge. Unfortunately, the Khmer Rouge had declared Buddhism a reactionary religion. By the time the Maoists had fled Phnom Penh, there were fewer than one hundred Khmer monks left, and they were living in exile. Despite being a communist nation, the PRK permitted Buddhism to return. The government allowed new monks to be ordained and temples to be restored. By 1981, approximately 1,500 novices had been ordained. An official report in 1982 mentioned that

---

[i] Chung, J. (2015, August 18). *In Cambodia, Clearing Landmines Brightens Futures.* Retrieved from Reliefweb.int: https://reliefweb.int/report/cambodia/cambodia-clearing-landmines-brightens-futures

[ii] Heder, D. S. (2007). *People's Republic of Kampuchea, 1979-1991.* Retrieved from Sophanseng.info: https://www.sophanseng.info/khmer-language-and-identity/peoples-republic-of-kampuchea-1979-1991

Cambodia had 2,311 monks. The government had to be careful because Marxists viewed religion as unhealthy. The PRK did its best to be sure that the restoration of Buddhism did not offend the Vietnamese, who were officially atheists.[i]

The regime also restored temples. There is no more significant cultural monument in Cambodia than Angkor Wat. The temple complex had been damaged because of fighting that took place around it, and Angkor Wat suffered structural damage in addition to the natural decay that occurred over the years. Walls needed repair, and elaborate carvings, a significant feature of the temples, required restoration work. The PRK's financial resources were limited, but it began the work that would bring this Cambodian masterpiece back from the brink. Other cultural improvements sponsored by the PRK were revivals of Cambodian theater and the artistic practices that the Khmer Rouge had suppressed.

Economic Improvements

Ten years of warfare and mismanagement had torn the Cambodian economy to shreds. Even though the Vietnamese army could be called upon for assistance, the PRK realized that its legitimacy in the minds and hearts of the Cambodian people would be jeopardized if economic revitalization did not happen.

Agriculture was an essential area for economic improvement. The PRK concentrated on reviving the rice harvest. That was critical because in 1979, only 800,000 tons of rice were produced. That was not sufficient to feed the population. Success came gradually, thanks to the government's efforts. The 1.6 million tons of rice were harvested in 1980, and that grew to 1.9 million tons in 1982. This was in spite of droughts and floods in the Mekong River Delta.[ii] Infrastructure projects to rebuild the roads and bridges that the Khmer Rouge had destroyed needed to be authorized.

Cambodia was recovering from the years of war, but the centralized control of the economy, which was a feature of communist countries, was not adequately helping Cambodia recover. In 1986, Vietnam

---

[i] Keyes, C. (2010, March 2). *Buddhism and Revolution in Cambodia.* Retrieved from Culturalsurvival.org: https://www.culturalsurvival.org/publications/cultural-survival-quarterly/buddhism-and-revolution-cambodia

[ii] Chufrin, G. I. (1984, November). *Five Years of the People's Revolutionary Power in Kampuchea.* Retrieved from Jstor.org: https://www.jstor.org/stable/2644148

introduced economic reforms to help invigorate its economy. Known as Doi Moi, a market economy was implemented in Vietnam. A limited amount of private enterprise was permitted, which resulted in a reduction in the levels of Vietnamese poverty. Similar efforts were tried in Cambodia. Private property rights were authorized, and state-owned companies were privatized in 1989. The results were very positive for the country's economy.

Rehabilitate the People

Cambodians were in desperate need of healing. Almost every family had suffered a loss because of forced labor and massacres. There was considerable rage that had to be addressed, or else the nation would collapse into anarchy. The government laid the blame for all of the problems at the Khmer Rouge's feet. Efforts were made to find the mass graves and dig up the remains so that families could properly bury their loved ones. Memorials were set up to recognize the human losses, and national days of remembrance were instituted to help people deal with their anger. The people were encouraged to tell their stories.[i]

An Isolated Country

The international community's ostracism of the PRK is an example of how the Cold War could sometimes be illogical. American President Jimmy Carter condemned the Khmer Rouge for its brutality. However, the American government also had no problem allowing the CDKG, the coalition that included the Khmer Rouge, to hold the Cambodian seat in the United Nations. The problem was that the PRK was officially a communist nation, and American foreign policy was hostile to communist regimes. The foreign aid that would have expedited the nation's recovery was denied, thanks to Cold War politics.

The irony is that even though the coalition of insurgents had non-communist members, the Khmer Rouge would have had no problem eliminating them if the PRK was ever overthrown. The Khmer Rouge considered the coalition nothing more than a means to an end. If ever given the chance, its members would go back to their old ways with even greater ferocity.

The PRK was a client state of Vietnam from 1979 to 1989. The control the Vietnamese had over the People's Republic of Kampuchea

---

[i] Vachon, M. (2017, April 21). *Healing a Nation.* Retrieved from English.cambodiadailycom: https://english.cambodiadaily.com/features/healing-a-nation-128377/

was comparable to the years of the French protectorate. The Cambodian government drew on the Vietnamese model for guidance. The Cambodian leadership was comprised of many former members of the Khmer Rouge who had escaped Vietnam and owed their jobs to the Vietnamese. Furthermore, they owed their lives to the Vietnamese because they would have been executed immediately if the Khmer Rouge ever came back into power. Vietnamese advisors were everywhere within the PRK's bureaucracy. Government decisions were consequently aligned with Vietnamese goals and objectives.

While the relationship with its eastern neighbor was sometimes uncomfortable, the people had no choice but to accept it. The Kampuchean People's Revolutionary Armed Forces (KPRAF) would not have been able to stand up to the enemies of the regime had it not been for the Vietnamese army. Thousands of Vietnamese troops were in Cambodia to help defend against the Khmer Rouge and other insurgents. The KPRAF was dependent on the Vietnamese for military assistance and training.

Critics contend that the Vietnamese exploited Cambodia's natural resources to help Vietnam's economy. While that might have been true, it was also true that the reconstruction of the roads, bridges, and other infrastructure happened under the direction of Vietnamese advisors. The People's Republic of Kampuchea would not have survived without the Vietnamese presence.

The Vietnamese Withdrawal

The Cambodian people resented foreign troops on their soil, even though the Vietnamese were actively helping the country. Vietnam was experiencing trouble because of the expenses incurred while maintaining a substantial number of troops in Cambodia. Moreover, Vietnam had its own problems to deal with, and the PRK was becoming a burden.

There was pressure from the international community for Vietnam to leave. China vigorously opposed the Vietnamese occupation of Cambodia and supplied aid to the insurgents. The tensions between Vietnam and China resulted in an international crisis on the China-Vietnam border, which resulted in military clashes. The Soviet Union was a major ally of Vietnam, and it, too, was pressing for a Vietnamese withdrawal. The reasons for staying in Cambodia were dwindling, and the Vietnamese investment of time, resources, and military support was beginning to receive diminishing returns. Was there a need to stay?

Not really. By the end of the 1980s, the PRK was in sufficient charge of affairs within Cambodia, and it did not have to rely so much on the help of the Vietnamese. It was time for a change. In a meeting of the National Assembly of the PRK held in late April 1989, the name of the country was changed to the State of Cambodia. Other changes included economic reforms, and the country was officially designated as a neutral, non-aligned state.

It was also decided that negotiations would be conducted with the opposition. The State of Cambodia continued with counterinsurgency operations, but peace negotiations with the opposition were held at the same time. There was no longer a pressing need for a foreign military presence, and the Vietnamese formally withdrew from Cambodia on September 26th, 1989.

Cambodia was finally free of foreign troops, but there was still much to do before the nation was completely sound. The question of what to do about the ongoing insurgency had to be successfully answered.

A firm lesson from the Holocaust was that those responsible for crimes against humanity must be held accountable. The Khmer Rouge had massacred innocent civilians and committed outrageous crimes against the Cambodian people when it was in power. The healing process in Cambodia would be incomplete if the criminals were not brought to justice. The Cambodian people were determined that there would be a reckoning.

Chapter 8 – Cambodia's Transition to Peace: The UNTAC Mission and Restoration of the Monarchy

International politics played a role in Vietnam's decision to leave Cambodia. The Soviet Union was in flux and could no longer provide support to the Vietnamese. Additionally, there was an international desire to rein in Vietnam's control of the Republic of Kampuchea and perhaps bring lasting peace to Southeast Asia, which had been in a state of military turmoil for nearly fifty years. It was essential to bring all of the parties to the table for negotiation. Each group had its own agenda.

The Khmer Rouge were the most belligerent. It was no secret that its members wanted to return to power in the country, and the Vietnamese withdrawal was an opportunity to gain a military victory. However, China was the primary supplier of the Khmer Rouge, and the Chinese wanted peace. The Khmer Rouge were brought to the table, however reluctantly, but they were suspicious of any settlement.

FUNCINPEC (the National United Front for an Independent, Neutral, Peaceful and Cooperative Cambodia) was headed by Norodom Sihanouk. This group's goal was to restore the monarchy to Cambodia. It was able to serve as a mediator and bring the Khmer Rouge and the other factions into meaningful dialogue.

The KPNLF (the Khmer People's National Liberation Front) was an anti-communist group that opposed both the Khmer Rouge and the State of Cambodia. It worked closely with FUNCINPEC.

The State of Cambodia hoped to stay in power and achieve international legitimacy. It would have to reconcile all of the opposing views at the negotiation table and, in some way, hammer out an agreement that everyone could live with. The main goal was to bring permanent peace to Cambodia.

The Stakeholders

The internal players in Cambodia were not the only ones who had a stake in the peace process. China and the United States were deeply concerned about the outcome of the negotiation efforts. In addition, the members of the Association of Southeast Asian Nations (ASEAN) wanted an end to the fighting. These countries had their own reasons and goals to pursue, and these outside interests were not always in sync with the negotiation process. The biggest problem was the need for more cooperation from the Khmer Rouge. They refused to lay down their arms, and they habitually broke ceasefires and truces.

The desire to get back on top was probably not the only reason the Khmer Rouge proved so stubborn. Evidence of their reign of terror was being uncovered on a routine basis, and the leaders of the Khmer Rouge might have been worried about accountability. It was enough that the Maoist radicals were being condemned by the international community. Legal action could be taken against all of them, and they did not want that.

The Role of the Peacemaker

A pivotal character in the negotiations was Norodom Sihanouk. The former king possessed considerable recognition both internationally and within Cambodia. As the head of FUNCINPEC, he was an active participant in all peace negotiations. He communicated with both the internal Cambodian factions and the international powers. He kept the conversation flowing even when there were sharp disagreements. Some remain skeptical of his role, but no one can doubt his prestige. His contributions were important factors in the final success of the peace process.

The Paris Peace Agreements

The bargaining and dealmaking finally produced the desired results. The comprehensive Cambodian peace agreements, the Paris Peace Agreements, were officially signed on October 23rd, 1991. The signatories were nineteen countries that were either Asian nations or had considerable interests in that part of the world.

Part of the Paris Peace Agreements gave the framework for peace in Cambodia and what steps were needed for a final settlement. The agreement on the political settlement of the Cambodian conflict outlined the establishment of a democratic government that would sponsor fair and free elections. The agreement concerning the sovereignty, territorial integrity, inviolability, neutrality, and national unity of Cambodia not only stressed the significance of Cambodia as a sovereign nation but also ensured that it would be a neutral country. Finally, the declaration of rehabilitation and reconstruction of Cambodia was put in place to assure that there would be international support in rebuilding Cambodia.[i]

The deal was signed, but now, a great deal of work was needed to ensure that Cambodia would finally be a peaceful nation free of internal turmoil and combat. The Khmer Rouge would continue to be a problem, but the international community was committed to seeing the peace agreements enforced. The United Nations became intimately involved in the efforts.

The international community recognized that peace could not be established in Cambodia without assistance. Accordingly, the United Nations Transitional Authority in Cambodia, UNTAC, was created to implement the Paris Peace Agreements. The process would not be easy, but the safety and sanity of the Cambodian people required that maximum effort be exerted to create a lasting peace.

The Mandate of UNTAC

UNTAC was tasked with safeguarding human rights in the country and monitoring any human rights abuses, which were also to be reported to the appropriate authorities. The ceasefire agreement meant the disarmament and demobilization of warring factions. UNTAC would be required to verify troop withdrawals and destroy confiscated weapons.

---

[i] United States Institute of Peace. (2000, February 22). *Peace Agreements: Cambodia.* Retrieved from Usip.org: https://www.usip.org/publications/2000/02/peace-agreements-cambodia.

The civil administration had to be properly restored within Cambodia as well. UNTAC was to ensure that the government was operating efficiently during the transitional period and that law and order prevailed. UNTAC was the head of a force of civilian police numbering 3,600, and they worked in cooperation with other units for pacification. Landmine removal and the repatriation of refugees were the most critical responsibilities of UNTAC.

Landmine Removal

Mine clearance was an essential duty. Those anti-personnel devices that had been placed throughout Cambodia needed to be located and destroyed. Significant minefields had to be marked, and the public needed to be aware of the existence of these hidden explosives.

These were not mines scattered here and there. Large tracts of land were dotted with these devices. Areas that could be used for farming had to be cleared of any danger. Human safety was at risk as long as the landmines were in place. Getting rid of them would allow Cambodians to move freely. It goes without saying that building roads and establishing hospitals and schools would be easier once the land was safe to walk on.

It would be a challenging task because there was still sporadic fighting. Dense vegetation had to be cleared for the mines to be removed. Equipment was scarce, and funding was needed. By the time the UNTAC mission was completed, over four million square miles of Cambodia had been cleared of mines, and approximately thirty-seven thousand mines and unexploded ordnance had been destroyed.[i]

Repatriation

It was the most sensitive assignment for UNTAC. Close to 365,000 Cambodian refugees were in refugee camps along the border of Thailand, and there were others elsewhere. UNTAC would oversee the repatriation and resettlement of these refugees and would work with international agencies to facilitate the return of these people to their homes. UNTAC would be involved in rebuilding Cambodia's infrastructure. There would also be safe and fair elections, as promised in the agreements.[ii]

---

[i] VanDeCarr, P. (2018, September 30). *How Cambodia Is Clearing Landmines to Rebuild Peace*. Retrieved from Govinsider.asia: https://govinsider.asia/intl-en/article/how-cambodia-is-clearing-landmines-to-rebuild-peace

[ii] Peacekeeping.un.org. (2024, December 28). *Cambodia-UNTAC*. Retrieved from

Repatriation would be very emotional. Thousands of Cambodians had fled their homes and were living in refugee camps in Thailand and Vietnam, hoping to one day return to their roots. Repatriated Cambodians would rebuild their communities, and the labor force would increase. Most importantly, devastated communities would once again be made whole. The challenges included adequate funding for repatriation and the availability of safe ground.[i]

Khmer Rouge Resistance

The Khmer Rouge would test the UNTAC's efforts to stabilize Cambodia. The former rulers of the country were suspicious of any outsiders and believed that, for all of its good intentions, UNTAC threatened their autonomy and position within Cambodia. These seasoned guerrilla fighters refused to lay down their arms and were not willing to comply with any ceasefire arrangement. The Khmer Rouge had a private agenda, and the Paris Peace Agreements would not get in their way.

This placed the United Nations in a problematic situation. The UN could not take military action against the Khmer Rouge because these guerrilla fighters were forces to be reckoned with. UNTAC left the Khmer Rouge alone in the areas of Cambodia they controlled.[ii]

UNTAC was sharply criticized for its passive dealings with the Khmer Rouge. Nevertheless, UNTAC was making progress with other parts of its mandate. A significant task lay ahead: the general elections. Success was critical for a peaceful Cambodia to survive.

The Elections

Yasushi Akashi was head of UNTAC from 1992 to 1993. His primary mission was to ensure that Cambodia would have a free and fair election as agreed upon in the Paris Peace Agreements. This was a monumental task with no guarantee of success.

Peacekeeping.un.org: https://peacekeeping.un.org/mission/past/untacbackgr2.html#six

[i] Michael W. Doyle, I. J. (2009, October 22). *Returning Home: Repatriation of Cambodian Refugees*. Retrieved from Cambridge.org: https://www.cambridge.org/core/books/abs/keeping-the-peace/returning-home-the-repatriation-of-cambodian-refugees/7F2D6C955AB0734D9EBF930D233AEB07

[ii] Greer, T. (2021, January 20). *The Forgotten UN Intervention to Build Democracy in Cambodia*. Retrieved from Palladium.com: https://www.palladiummag.com/2021/01/20/the-forgotten-un-intervention-to-build-democracy-in-cambodia/

The biggest obstacle on the road to the ballot box was the Khmer Rouge. Its members decided to boycott the election because their official reason was that the country lacked a politically neutral atmosphere. A more realistic justification was that the Khmer Rouge were afraid that the election would underscore their unpopularity and show the resistance of the Cambodian people to allowing the Khmer Rouge to participate in any legitimate government. The Khmer Rouge did what they could to disrupt the election process. They interfered with UNTAC activities and attacked the offices of the opposition parties.

The Khmer Rouge tried to stop UNTAC from operating in rural areas by refusing to let the United Nations into large parts of the countryside. However, they weren't the only ones causing violence. The State of Cambodia, worried about losing support to more conservative groups, attacked the offices of non-communist parties. Part of what fueled the violence was how easy it was to get weapons. UNTAC couldn't fully disarm the different factions. Many of the weapons they collected didn't even work properly.[i]

Voter registration was impeded by Cambodia's faulty infrastructure. Transportation still needed improvement, and landmines were disrupting attempts to reach all areas of the country. The most important question to be answered by the elections is whether these would produce the desired results of a new country that was recognized by all of its citizens.

The Election of a New Cambodia

Elections were held between May 23rd and May 28th, 1993, to allow people in outlying areas to cast their votes. UNTAC supervised all election activity. There was still the danger of violence, and Khmer Rouge guerrillas actively disrupted the voting. Yasushi Akashi and his UNTAC colleagues could do nothing more than watch and hold their breath, hoping for the best. The results of the election astounded everybody.

In spite of the dangers, the Cambodian people came out in droves to vote. The voter turnout was approximately 89.56 percent of all eligible voters. FUNCINPEC received the most votes, securing 45 percent of the

---

[i] Parida, S. (2020, August). *Case Analysis of the Cambodian Elections of 1993 and 1998.* Retrieved from Researchgate.net:
https://www.researchgate.net/publication/344202929_Case_Analysis_of_the_Cambodian_Elections_of_1993_and_1998

overall vote and winning 58 seats in the 120-member constituent assembly. The Cambodia People's Party (CPP) came in second with 38 percent of the vote. Democracy had won a significant victory in a land that had known nothing but dissension and turmoil for over twenty years.

The New Government

FUNCINPEC had won, but the Cambodian People's Party refused to acknowledge the victory. It accused the United Nations of massive fraud and threatened to increase violence. The only way to legitimize the election would be to compromise. A power-sharing arrangement was brokered by Norodom Sihanouk. There would be a coalition government with co-prime ministers, Prince Norodom Ranariddh (Sihanouk's son) and Hun Sen, a former Khmer Rouge defector who had served as prime minister since 1985 under the Vietnamese-backed government. There were people who were disappointed in the arrangement because it allowed the Cambodian People's Party, of which Hun Sen was a part, to have control over the military and administrative functions of the country. The Khmer Rouge refused to recognize the validity of the election, but that was expected.[i]

Disagreements over the validity of the outcome notwithstanding, the elections were a major development in Cambodia. Nearly everyone who was qualified to vote participated, and it could not be denied that a government was being formed that would reflect a change in direction for Cambodia. The country had witnessed years of brutal repression and near anarchy. There was now light at the end of the tunnel, and the Cambodians were marching toward it. The Khmer Rouge continued to be a nuisance in Cambodia, but despite all of their rhetoric, the elections showed Cambodia's collective intent. The people had spoken.

Return of the King

The end of a monarchy is not always permanent. The Bourbon dynasty in France was restored after the fall of Napoleon Bonaparte, and the Spanish monarchy was reinstated upon the death of Francisco Franco. What is most important is that the good of the country is the primary reason for putting a king back on the throne.

The Khmer Rouge had rejected the election results, and there was a critical need to unify the country. The Paris Peace Agreements had

---

[i] Ebrary.net. (2024, December 28). *The Cambodian Elections of 1993*. Retrieved from Ebrary.net: https://ebrary.net/33668/political_science/cambodian_elections_1993

called for the restoration of the monarchy in a transitional government, which was having difficulties governing the country. Norodom Sihanouk was seen as the only person deemed capable of taking on the role of king. On June 14th, 1993, Sihanouk was reinstated in his old job as head of state by Cambodia's Constituent Assembly. The new king made a few cosmetic changes, such as renaming the Cambodian military the Royal Cambodian Armed Forces and renaming the country once again; this time, it would be called the Kingdom of Cambodia.

Norodom Ranariddh and Hun Sen would continue as co-prime ministers, and Cabinet positions would be divided between the CPP and FUNCINPEC. Sihanouk was a constitutional monarch, but he had limited powers. His role, however, was important. Despite all the years of turmoil and chaos, he remained a highly respected person in the eyes of the Cambodian people. Sihanouk was a symbol of the past and the unifying figure for the Cambodian nation.

Norodom Sihanouk and his wife, Monineath.[18]

There was much to do for the new government. The work of rebuilding Cambodia was still ongoing, and the repatriation of refugees resulted in high unemployment. The government tried to revitalize the economy and find a place in the workforce for the returning people. The Khmer Rouge continued to be a threat as well. Sihanouk's efforts at reconciliation were rebuffed, and the king of Cambodia was forced to continue military operations against the insurgents.

Why did the Khmer Rouge continue to resist even though it was clear the Cambodian people wanted a constitutional monarchy? One reason was the steadfast commitment to the ideals of the group, which encouraged the Khmer Rouge to continue fighting. The new government, in their eyes, was nothing more than a puppet for foreign interests. The leadership of what was left of the Khmer Rouge was still influential and had complete control over the members. This internal cohesion committed the Khmer Rouge to continue the fight even though the odds were stacked against them.

The Khmer Rouge was still receiving some international support, but this gradually decreased over time. The organization still had control of remote areas, but it was becoming clear that the days of the Khmer Rouge as a political influence in Cambodia were over.

The Reconciliation Process

The atrocities committed by the Khmer Rouge were a seeping wound that needed to be healed. It was not going to be easy because so many Cambodians had suffered and lost family members and friends to the Pol Pot regime. Nevertheless, something had to be done to end the lingering problem of what to do with the Khmer Rouge.

Restorative justice was one path forward. The government could find the truth and expose it to the public. Many former Khmer Rouge members, especially low-ranking members, were encouraged to accept responsibility and express remorse rather than face formal prosecution. The tribunal's approach prioritized collective moral reparations (like memorials and education initiatives) over individual monetary compensation. However, senior leaders were formally tried and sentenced to life in prison.

There is a tendency for reconciliation to try to forget what happened completely. That is not always possible because memories of injustice still linger on. Remembrance helps a victim in the healing process. The memorials and days of remembrance that were instituted were outward signs of a nation keeping in mind what had been officially done to innocent people. Because a generation of Cambodians had grown up without knowing about the Khmer Rouge, education was necessary.

Finally, proactive healing in the form of therapy and counseling would help individuals heal. All of these actions would require time to be implemented and to generate results. Cambodia would have to start the reconciliation process amid the need for economic development in a country that was overwhelmed by poverty, thanks to years of war.[i]

Death of a Monster

Pol Pot died on April 15th, 1998, in an area along the Cambodia-Thailand border. He had no remorse at the time of his death for all the deeds he had done. In fact, he claimed that his actions had been for the good of the country. He died with no regrets for the crimes against humanity that had been committed. He never faced justice for what he had done either; however, he stands accused and convicted before the bar of history.

There were efforts to bring the Khmer Rouge soldiers back into general Cambodian society that included embassy programs and a willingness to allow Khmer Rouge members to be a part of the civil service. Unfortunately, there were delays in setting up a judicial process for punishing the most extreme criminals of the Pol Pot regime. The death of the former dictator robbed the Khmer Rouge movement of its primary figure. Additionally, the demise of Pol Pot spurred the international community to persuade Cambodia to be more resolute in bringing the other Khmer Rouge leaders to justice before they also died.

Extraordinary Chambers in the Courts of Cambodia

The Extraordinary Chambers in the Courts of Cambodia (ECCC) was created on January 2nd, 2001, to prosecute the senior leaders of the Khmer Rouge. These men would be charged with crimes against humanity, attempted genocide, and various war crimes. The ECCC was a Cambodian version of the Nuremberg trials. The court would take the victim statements of nearly four thousand victims during formal proceedings that were conducted from 2006 to 2022.

---

[i] Estelle Bockers, M.S. (2022, November). *Reconciliation in Cambodia: Thirty Years After the Terror of the Khmer Rouge Regime*. Retrieved from Trct.org: https://irct.org/wp-content/uploads/2022/11/Volume-21-No.-2.pdf

The leaders who were brought to trial included the following:
- Kaing Guek Eav was the man placed in charge of the Tuol Sleng prison. He was found guilty in 2010 and sentenced to thirty-five years in prison, which was later changed to life imprisonment. He died in 2020.
- Nuon Chea was the second-in-command of the Khmer Rouge. He was convicted of crimes against humanity in 2014 and later of genocide in 2018. His sentence was life imprisonment, and he died while serving his term.
- Khieu Samphan's title was head of state of Democratic Kampuchea. He was convicted of crimes against humanity in 2014. In 2018, he was convicted of genocide. He was sentenced to life imprisonment, and as of this writing, he is still serving his sentence.
- Ieng Saru was the deputy prime minister and minister of foreign affairs. He was charged with crimes against humanity and genocide, but he died in 2013 before the court could reach a verdict.
- Ieng Thirith was the highest-ranking female leader in the Khmer Rouge and was the minister of social affairs. Although she was charged with crimes against humanity and genocide, she was declared unfit to be tried because of Alzheimer's disease. She died in 2015.

These were the senior leaders of the Khmer Rouge. One criticism of the ECCC was that mid-level and lower-ranking Khmer Rouge members were not tried at all. Furthermore, four Khmer Rouge leaders remained involved in Cambodian politics, and the government did not want to have them tried.

The Extraordinary Chambers in the Courts of Cambodia issued a final decision in 2022 and completed the judicial proceedings. Although it has been criticized for not doing more, the ECCC left behind more than two million pages of historically significant documents, which include tens of thousands of records and over 1,300 judicial decisions. It played a major role in defining the crimes and atrocities committed by the Khmer Rouge against the Cambodian people. It was a prodigious effort that has helped in the rehabilitation of a shattered country.[i]

---

[i] ECCC.gov. (2024, December 28). *The Extraordinary Chambers in the Courts of Cambodia.* Retrieved from ECCC.gov: https://www.eccc.gov.kh/en

Chapter 9 - Reconstruction and Progress in the Twenty-First Century

If a Cambodian Rip Van Winkle went to sleep in 1979 and woke up today, that person would be awestruck by the change. Cambodia today is nowhere near what it was when the Pol Pot regime collapsed. It took a great deal of determination, perseverance, and willingness to sacrifice, but the nation is now a model of rehabilitation.

Cambodia is a significant contributor to international society. Improvements have been in every segment of society and the economy. What has happened is nothing short of a miracle that the Cambodian people themselves created.

Economic Development

Improvements occurred in several key sectors of Cambodia's economy. The garment and footwear industry is the primary part of Cambodia's manufacturing sector. Eighty percent of exports in 2022 were garments and footwear. Cambodia's success is based on preferential trade agreements, a large workforce, and low labor costs. Exports mushroomed from $962 million in 2000 to $12.6 billion in 2022. While the 2020 pandemic did cause temporary drops in export figures, they have since rebounded.

Electronics and electrical appliances had nonexistent export figures in 2012. However, in 2022, this part of the Cambodian economy exported approximately $2 billion worth of products. Automotive parts are becoming a growth area for Cambodians.

The major challenges for Cambodia's manufacturing sector are a shortage of skilled workers, an electricity grid that does not adequately cover the rural areas of the country, and a highway system that needs work. Efforts are being made to correct all of these problems as Cambodia moves forward.[i]

Tourism

Jayavarman VII could not have imagined the enormity of the gift he gave to Cambodia's future when he was building Angkor Wat. The temple complex is the cornerstone of a vibrant tourist industry in Cambodia. In 2022, Cambodia had 2.2 million international visitors. Most of these guests were from Vietnam, Thailand, and China. Revenue from tourism has gone from 9.44 percent of Cambodia's gross domestic product in 2000 to 19.61 percent in 2019.

Efforts are being made to expand tourism into other areas besides Angkor Wat. Tourists typically spend around seven days in the country, and Cambodia's desire is to increase the vacation days per tourist so that more money is spent inside the country. Once again, the poor infrastructure is a challenge that the Cambodian government has to overcome as quickly as possible.[ii]

Agriculture

Agriculture is the traditional powerhouse of Cambodia's economy and continues to be a major business sector. Increases in agricultural gross production have enabled Cambodia's poverty levels to drop, and increased yields brought on by mechanization have helped. Rice production has flattened out in recent years, and the environmental sustainability of farming has to be strengthened. Nevertheless, considerable opportunity is still being found in Cambodia's fields.[iii]

---

[i] B2B Cambodia. (2024, February 6). *Cambodia's Manufacturing Sector: Opportunities and Challenges in 2024.* Retrieved from b2b-cambodia.com: https://b2b-cambodia.com/news/cambodias-manufacturing-sector-opportunities-and-challenges-in-2024/

[ii] *Tourism.* (2023, February 2). Retrieved from Opendevelopmentcambodiaa.net: https://opendevelopmentcambodia.net/topics/tourism/

[iii] Worldbank.org. (2024, December 29). *Cambodian Agriculture in Transition: Opportunities and Risks.* Retrieved from Worldbank.org: https://www.worldbank.org/en/country/cambodia/publication/cambodian-agriculture-in-transition-opportunities-and-risks

Poverty Reduction in Cambodia

Poverty was once an unpleasant fact of life in Cambodia, and there did not seem to be any chance of that improving. However, the World Bank report, "Cambodia Poverty Assessment 2022: Toward a More Inclusive and Resilient Cambodia," indicates that there has been amazing progress in bringing down the poverty levels in Cambodia. Cambodia's national poverty rate fell nearly half between 2009 and 2019, and this was due in part to rapid economic growth that increased labor earnings and reduced poverty. Living standards improved, and the overall success in growth and poverty reduction was aided by macroeconomic stability and prudent fiscal management.

A problem that many developing countries encounter is that profits end up in the hands of only a few people while the rest of the population remains poor. This does not appear to be the case in Cambodia, which has high employment rates and income growth. Furthermore, the economy has diversified away from agriculture into manufacturing and tourism so that a person's income is not dependent on the success of a harvest.[i]

Investments in Human Capital

Modern societies increasingly depend more on intellectual capacity than muscle to get the job done. Human capital needs to be developed and enhanced to allow a country to succeed. Cambodia recognized the importance of human capital investments and has made great strides in the 21st century to foster that growth.

Teacher training and professional development have been two essential objectives. Teachers in the rural areas of Cambodia must have ongoing training to enhance the quality of their lessons and knowledge. Primary school enrollment exceeds the world average in Cambodia, although problems with secondary school enrollment remain. The rural areas are a particular concern because of higher dropout rates. Cambodia has made scholarships, meals, and programs for special needs students so that every Cambodian child has an opportunity to learn.

---

[i] Worldbank.org. (2022, November 28). *Cambodia Poverty Assessment 2022: Toward a More Inclusive and Resilient Cambodia.* Retrieved from Worldbank.org:
https://www.worldbank.org/en/country/cambodia/publication/cambodia-poverty-assessment-2022-toward-a-more-inclusive-and-resilient-cambodia

Government projects, including the General Education Improvement Project, have addressed school infrastructure, upgraded school buildings, and provided upgraded learning materials to increase students' learning capacities.

Academic classes are important, but Cambodia understands that vocational training is essential to help people survive in the modern world too. Vocational training pathways are explored in upper secondary schools, and partnerships with private sector firms are helping to enhance workforce training and certification.

The greatest challenge to education is in Cambodia's rural areas, as we mentioned. Improvements are still needed in infrastructure and access to learning in remote areas. However, the country is doing everything possible to ensure that no child is left behind due to a lack of access to qualified teachers, modern schools, and a curriculum that challenges the students and prepares them for working life.[i]

Culture and Heritage

Preserving culture and restoring heritage means more than developing attractive tourist locations. The Cambodian people suffered immensely in the latter half of the 20th century. The excesses of the Khmer Rouge regime harmed the people's self-esteem and pride. Restoring Cambodia's culture and heritage allows the citizens to once again have a sense of pride in being Cambodian. The nation has worked diligently to restore what has been damaged and to cultivate the culture of Cambodia.

The most significant work has been on the restoration of buildings. This is not just Angkor Wat. UNESCO sites like the temple of Preah Vihear and the Temple Zone of Sambor Prei Kuk were damaged during the war and need restoration work. Looting has been a serious problem, and greater security measures are being enforced to protect Cambodia's treasures. Foreign countries have helped in the efforts. The United States has given millions of dollars in aid to assist in preserving cultural sites and protecting them from thieves.[ii]

---

[i] Educationcambodia.org. (2024, January 16). *Education in Cambodia: Progress, Challenges, and Opportunities*. Retrieved from Educationcambodia.org:
https://educationcambodia.org/education-cambodia-progress-challenges-opportunities/22332/

[ii] Willis, C. C. (2023, October 2). *Protecting Cambodia's Cultural Heritage: US-Cambodia Conservation Ties*. Retrieved from Asiamattersforamerica.org:
https://asiamattersforamerica.org/articles/protecting-cambodias-cultural-heritage-us-cambodia-conservation-ties

Today, traditional arts are honored in Cambodia, and festivals celebrating heritage are part of the social landscape. These have all helped Cambodians develop a greater appreciation and respect for the unique culture of their country, which dates back centuries.[i]

Transition of the Government

Cambodia is no longer the pariah nation it was under the Khmer Rouge. It is now a member of the ASEAN and joined the World Trade Organization (WTO) in 2004. Unfortunately, there are still issues regarding how Cambodia is governed that must be addressed.

It became a monarchy in 1993 when a coalition between the Cambodian People's Party (CPP) and the FUNCINPEC party existed. However, in 1997, a coup d'état occurred in which one co-prime minister, Hun Sen, ousted the other co-prime minister, Norodom Ranariddh. Hun Sen was declared the sole prime minister on November 30th, 1998, and went on to win the next three elections.

Hun Sen.[14]

---

[i] Davidson, J. (2024, May 16). *Preserving Cambodian Culture and Heritage through Cultural Education and Preservation.* Retrieved from Acodo.org: https://acodo.org/preserving-cambodian-culture-and-heritage-through-cultural-education-and-preservation/

Hun Sen has been described as a "tiger that rules the mountain." He had a reputation for using unethical means to maintain an authoritarian regime in Cambodia. Due to a number of inter-party alliances, he kept the CPP firmly in his control. He was not above nepotism, as his relatives held important positions in the police and army. Hun Sen has been accused of manipulating elections and misusing public funds. He could be ruthless when dealing with political opponents and has tried to undermine the opposition whenever possible.

Nevertheless, this man cannot be compared to Pol Pot. Hun Sen recognized the importance of economic improvement as a way to maintain his power. Cambodia experienced a commercial renaissance under Hun Sen, and improvements were made to infrastructure. He maintained good international ties with other countries, which have helped in the economic improvement of Cambodia. His record on civil rights was not a good one, but the mass murders and oppression of the Khmer Rouge were far worse.

Hun Sen was one of the longest-ruling heads of state in the world when he stepped down as prime minister on August 10th, 2023. He was succeeded by his son, Hun Manet. This does not mean that Hun Sen is completely retired. He continues to be the head of the CPP, at least as of this writing. How Hun Manet will govern Cambodia is still being developed, but it appears that he and his father have decided that Cambodia will be run under hegemonic authoritarian rule. This means there will still be elections, but they might not be totally fair. There will continue to be control over the media, and political opposition will experience intimidation tactics. Power is in the hands of the leader or the ruling party. Under this type of semi-dictatorship, Cambodia will continue to develop so that poverty will be reduced, and the middle class will be encouraged. The image is comparable to an iron fist covered by a velvet glove. It remains to be seen how this type of governance will ultimately benefit Cambodia in the future.[i]

It has been fifty years since the Khmer Rouge took control of Cambodia. The recovery is still an ongoing mission even though the ECCC closed its books in 2022. People need to look at the figures to better understand why Cambodia's rehabilitation is taking so long.

---

[i] Strangio, S. (2023, September 19). *Cambodia's Hun Sen: The Tiger That Rules the Mountain.* Retrieved from Thediplomat.com: https://thediplomat.com/2023/09/cambodias-hun-sen-the-tiger-that-rules-the-mountain/

Between 1975 and 1979, the Khmer Rouge killed approximately 25 percent of the Cambodian population. That does not include the millions who suffered from deprivation and starvation. There are many people still suffering from posttraumatic stress disorder and others mourning the loss of loved ones. A way to keep this in perspective is that the Holocaust ended eighty years ago, and there is still ongoing remembrance work. To forget and move on is not the way to deal with human catastrophes.

The recovery effort in Cambodia is occurring on several fronts.

Education

A generation of Cambodians has grown up not having experienced what the Khmer Rouge did. It is important to inform them since over 60 percent of Cambodia's population is under the age of thirty. To make certain that younger citizens are aware of what happened, Cambodia has undertaken educational efforts that share information about the atrocities.

There are mobile education buses that are equipped with projectors and touch screens to bring history to those students who live in farming communities. These vehicles also offer testimonies from the victims of the killing fields. The Public Genocide Education Forum distributes textbooks and encourages a dialogue to educate younger people about this dark era in Cambodia's history. The Tuol Sleng prison is now a museum, and the Choeung Ek killing fields are places that can be visited by those looking for education about what the Khmer Rouge did.[i]

Psychological Support and Therapy

Those who survived the horror cannot forget it. These people may still be living with the trauma of what happened to them and how it affected their lives. It is not easy to forget. The Transcultural Psychosocial Organization (TPO) was created to help survivors deal with the psychological damage. The target groups of this organization are the survivors, their families, and their communities. Its services include counseling, trauma treatment, and mental health services.

The ECCC sought to help people seek the truth, and psychological support services were offered to those who were witnesses. Testimonial

---

[i] Yonetici. (2024, August 24). *Bringing History to Life: Educating Cambodian Youth on the Khmer Rouge*. Retrieved from Balert.org: https://balert.org/2024/08/24/bringing-history-to-life-educating-cambodian-youth-on-the-khmer-rouge-genocide/

therapy is a means of allowing survivors to share their experiences to help them with the treatment of posttraumatic stress disorder. The TPO provides the opportunity for testimonial therapy for survivors. There are community-based therapy programs that have group counseling sessions for survivors as well.[i]

Community Reconciliation

Museums and historical sites remind people of what happened, and materials are archived that give the community a historical record of the Khmer Rouge nightmare. These can help future generations fully appreciate what took place. Cambodia encourages discussion and dialogue. Survivors are allowed to share their stories in the communities where they live. The community is engaged in open discussions about the Khmer Rouge years with the intent to foster a mutual support system within a population to help survivors better cope with their terrible memories.

Kdei Karuna is a nongovernmental organization that addresses reconciliation efforts. Gender-based violence was one of the tactics used by the Khmer Rouge to keep the people under their control. The Pka Slaa Project is one of the organization's programs to help heal those who were victims of forced marriage. Kdei Karuna takes advantage of mobile exhibitions and educational outreach to raise public awareness about forced marriages, and the organization provides a platform that enables survivors to share their stories.[ii]

Cambodia partners with international organizations to tell the story of the Khmer Rouge, but Cambodia is willing to go one step further. There are other nations that have experienced large-scale atrocities, such as Rwanda. Cambodia provides information on its experiences and how the country deals with the legacies of trauma.

There remain some obstacles to the complete rehabilitation of Cambodia's psyche. The young people of Cambodia have no connection with what happened, and efforts must continue to develop a collective memory that includes their recognition of what the Khmer Rouge did. Not all Cambodians feel that their recoveries have been

---

[i] Tpocambodia.org. (2024, December 29). *Promoting Healing & Reconciliation Through Psychosocial Interventions*. Retrieved from Tpocambodia.org: https://tpocambodia.org/promoting-healing-and-reconciliation/

[ii] Kdei-karuna.org. (2024, August 23). *Kdei Karuna Envisions an Inclusive Peaceful Society*. Retrieved from Kdei-Karuna.org: https://www.kdei-karuna.org/#main

adequately addressed. This is especially true in the rural areas of the country. Some of the veterans of the Khmer Rouge are still actively involved in Cambodian politics, which makes the discussion about the old regime highly sensitive. Nevertheless, Cambodia continues an ongoing effort of reconciliation and truth. Its efforts are a guide to other nations on how to manage the aftermath of mass terror.

The Death of an Icon

King Norodom Sihanouk died on October 15th, 2012. His son, Norodom Sihamoni, succeeded him as king. In a life that spanned nearly one century, Sihanouk was the dominant figure in 20th-century Cambodian history. No one came close to him when it came to influencing the course of history in the nation.

When Norodom Sihanouk came to the throne, he was only eighteen years old, and Cambodia was a protectorate of France. The French probably expected that he would be little more than a puppet or a playboy prince, spending most of his time living a life of comfort and pleasure. They were mistaken.

Norodom Sihanouk was a primary force in establishing an independent Cambodia and remained the principal decision-maker until he was ousted in 1970. Before that, he had been able to successfully keep Cambodia a neutral and independent state. Throughout the ups and downs of his life, he was revered by the Cambodian people. The title pater patriae ("father of the homeland") is a fitting description of this remarkable man.

Sihanouk's legacy justifiably deserves criticism because of his involvement in the Khmer Rouge. Pol Pot led a ragtag band of insurgents in the remote countryside without a chance of doing much better than that. Sihanouk's association with the Khmer Rouge permitted that group the credibility to recruit thousands of volunteers in the countryside and receive military assistance from other countries. It is possible that Sihanouk had no idea who he was dealing with at the beginning. He suppressed the Khmer Rouge for years and might have believed they were nothing to worry about. Why did everything go wrong?

History does not always repeat itself. Situations will, and that is why it is important to study the past carefully. A good analogy is comparing Pol Pot to Adolf Hitler just before the two came to power. Hitler had written the book *Mein Kampf*, and this text had been lampooned and ridiculed by the intelligentsia and world leaders as a rambling piece of nonsense. However, Hitler wrote about what he intended to do when he finally came to power in Germany. History tells us that the German dictator came very close to doing what he said he would do.

Pol Pot was a dedicated Maoist. He believed strongly in Chairman Mao's commitment to a revolution rising from the peasantry. This meant that city dwellers were not very important and could be viewed with a fair amount of suspicion. Sihanouk failed to understand how far the leader of the Khmer Rouge was willing to go to change Cambodian society. The former king might have believed that Pol Pot would be a little more realistic once in power and tone down his rhetoric. It was no doubt a shock to Sihanouk that the revolutionary was serious and meant every word about radically transforming the Cambodian people.

Sihanouk's alliance with the Khmer Rouge did not harm his image in the minds of the Cambodian people, though. Sihanouk would rise like the phoenix from the ashes and be king once again. He was able to mediate disputes in Cambodia largely because of his preeminence as a public figure. He abdicated in 2004 but still continued to be active until his death.

He was a great man in spite of his mistakes. When he became king, Cambodia was nothing but a piece of French property. It is now one of the fastest-growing economies in the world.

Conclusion

We know about the past and are aware of the present, but the future is always a tantalizing mystery. We cannot be sure what Cambodia's future will be, but there are some indications and noticeable trends that can give us some idea of what we might expect.

The CPP will continue to have a firm grip on the political life of Cambodia. It is unlikely that Hun Manet is going to go down a different route than his father, and there may be some reforms, but these will probably be incremental. There is no firm political opposition currently in Cambodia, and that situation will remain in the foreseeable future.

The economic development in Cambodia is going to continue. It is anticipated that Cambodia's current status as a least developed country will be gone by 2030, and current investments in ports and energy generation will enhance export trade and enable Cambodia to branch out into other areas of manufacturing besides the garment industry. Cambodia is part of China's Belt and Road Initiative, and China has invested heavily in Cambodia's highways and overall infrastructure. That relationship will likely continue.

The social divide in Cambodia could be a serious problem. The Khmer Rouge was able to recruit thousands of farmers who were dissatisfied with Cambodia's urban elite. The government has to be sure that economic development significantly affects the rural areas, reducing poverty and creating permanent employment, if it wants to keep the farmers happy.

One demographic that could bring about significant change both in government and society is the country's young people. The majority of the population is under the age of thirty, and they may want to see significant changes in the coming years. It is possible that the Cambodian government may relax some of its restrictions because of pressure from the youth.

Cambodia has endured adversity, particularly in the 20th century, that few nations have experienced. They were originally exploited by the French, bombed by the Americans, massacred by the Khmer Rouge, and overrun by the Vietnamese. Yet, in spite of such difficulties, the nation survived. Cambodians have a history of being knocked down and then rising again to face new challenges.

The resilience of these people is impressive. The core of the Cambodians' national character is the pride they have in their history. The Khmer Empire was a significant power in Southeast Asia centuries ago, and there are reminders of that brilliant age all throughout the country. An ability to endure hardship defines its modern identity. The country is well on its way to becoming an economic power in the region. This is in spite of being nearly destroyed fifty years ago.

The Cambodians have accomplished great things throughout the course of their history. There is every reason to anticipate that this proud nation of strong people will continue to survive and thrive in the years to come.

Here's another book by Enthralling History that you might like

Free limited time bonus

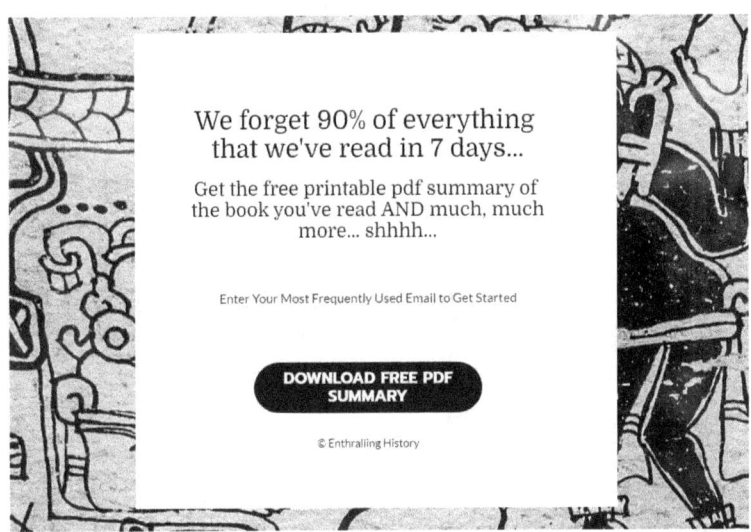

Stop for a moment. We have a free bonus set up for you. The problem is this: we forget 90% of everything that we read after 7 days. Crazy fact, right? Here's the solution: we've created a printable, 1-page pdf summary for this book that you're reading now. All you have to do to get your free pdf summary is to go to the following website: https://livetolearn.lpages.co/enthrallinghistory/

Or, Scan the QR code!

Once you do, it will be intuitive. Enjoy, and thank you!

Bibliography

Agatetravel.com. (2024, December 1). *Angkor Wat Architecture*. Retrieved from Agatetravel.com: https://www.agatetravel.com/angkor-wat-architecture.html.

Archives.gov. (2024, December 15). *Episode 9: Crossing into Cambodia*. Retrieved from Archives.gov: https://www.archives.gov/exhibits/remembering-vietnam-online-exhibit-episodes-9-12.

B2B Cambodia. (2024, February 6). *Cambodia's Manufacturing Sector: Opportunities and Challenges in 2024*. Retrieved from b2b-cambodia.com: https://b2b-cambodia.com/news/cambodias-manufacturing-sector-opportunities-and-challenges-in-2024/.

Bower, B. (2019, February 25). *Ancient Angkor's Mysterious Decline May Have Been Slow, Not Sudden*. Retrieved from Sciencenews.org: https://www.sciencenews.org/article/ancient-angkor-mysterious-decline-slow-not-sudden.

Cambodiatribunal.org. (2024, December 16). *Khmer Rouge History*. Retrieved from Cambodiatribunal.org: https://cambodiatribunal.org/history/cambodian-history/khmer-rouge-history/.

CENGAGE. (2018, June 27). *Sihanoul, Norodom*. Retrieved from Encyclopedia.com: https://www.encyclopedia.com/people/history/southeast-asia-history-biographies/norodom-sihanouk.

Chandler, D. P. (2024, July 18). *Tai and Vietnamese Hegemony*. Retrieved from Britannica.com: https://www.britannica.com/topic/history-of-Cambodia/Tai-and-Vietnamese-hegemony.

Chufrin, G. I. (1984, November). *Five Years of the People's Revolutionary Power in Kampuchea*. Retrieved from Jstor.org: https://www.jstor.org/stable/2644148.

Chung, J. (2015, August 18). *In Cambodia, Clearing Landmines Brightens Futures*. Retrieved from Reliefweb.int: https://reliefweb.int/report/cambodia/cambodia-clearing-landmines-brightens-futures.

Davidson, J. (2024, May 16). *Preserving Cambodian Culture and Heritage through Cultural Education and Preservation*. Retrieved from Acodo.org: https://acodo.org/preserving-cambodian-culture-and-heritage-through-cultural-education-and-preservation/.

Ebrary.net. (2024, December 28). *The Cambodian Elections of 1993*. Retrieved from Ebrary.net: https://ebrary.net/33668/political_science/cambodian_elections_1993.

ECCC.gov. (2024, December 28). *The Extraordinary Chambers in the Courts of Cambodia*. Retrieved from ECCC.gov: https://www.eccc.gov.kh/en.

Educationcambodia.org. (2024, January 16). *Education in Cambodia: Progress, Challenges, and Opportunities*. Retrieved from Educationcambodia.org: https://educationcambodia.org/education-cambodia-progress-challenges-opportunities/22332/.

Estelle Bockers, M.S. (2022, November). *Reconciliation in Cambodia: Thirty Years After the Terror of the Khmer Rouge Regime*. Retrieved from Trct.org: https://irct.org/wp-content/uploads/2022/11/Volume-21-No.-2.pdf.

Factsanddetails.com. (2014, May). *Cambodia under King Sihanouk*. Retrieved from Factsanddetails.com: https://factsanddetails.com/southeast-asia/Cambodia/sub5_2a/entry-2847.html.

Factsanddetails.com. (2014, May). *French Colonial Period in Cambodia*. Retrieved from Factsanddetails.com: https://factsanddetails.com/southeast-asia/Cambodia/sub5_2a/entry-2846.html.

Factsanddeteails.com. (2024, December 1). *Ancient Civilizations in Cambodia: Funan and Champa and the Chams*. Retrieved from FactsandDetails.com: https://factsanddetails.com/southeast-asia/Cambodia/sub5_2a/entry-2839.html.

Glass, A. (2015, November 18). *Nixon Asks Congress to Fund Aid for Cambodia, Nov. 18, 1970*. Retrieved from Politico.com: https://www.politico.com/story/2015/11/nixon-asks-congress-to-fund-aid-for-cambodia-nov-18-1970-215912.

Greer, T. (2021, January 20). *The Forgotten UN Intervention to Build Democracy in Cambodia*. Retrieved from Palladium.com: https://www.palladiummag.com/2021/01/20/the-forgotten-un-intervention-to-build-democracy-in-cambodia/.

Heder, D. S. (2007). *People's Republic of Kampuchea, 1979-1991*. Retrieved from Sophanseng.info: https://www.sophanseng.info/khmer-language-and-identity/peoples-republic-of-kampuchea-1979-1991/.

Ibcworld.org. (2024, December 1). *Buddhism Around the World.* Retrieved from Ibcworld.org: https://www.ibcworld.org/home/diaspora/Cambodia.

Jojo. (2024, December 1). *Social Structure.* Retrieved from Angkorempiretj.weebly.com: https://angkorempiretj.weebly.com/social-structure.html.

Kalyanaraman, S. (2018). *Processes of Indianization in the Khmer Empire.* Retrieved from Angkordatabase.asia: https://angkordatabase.asia/publications/processes-of-indianization-in-the-khmer-empire.

Kdei-karuna.org. (2024, August 23). *Kdei Karuna Envisions an Inclusive Peaceful Society.* Retrieved from Kdei-Karuna.org: https://www.kdei-karuna.org/#main.

Keyes, C. (2010, March 2). *Buddhism and Revolution in Cambodia.* Retrieved from Culturalsurvival.org: https://www.culturalsurvival.org/publications/cultural-survival-quarterly/buddhism-and-revolution-cambodia.

Khmerknowledgekeepers.weekly.com. (2025, January 1). *Welcome to the Khmer Knowledge Keepers' History of the Khmer Empire.* Retrieved from Khmerknowledgekeepers.weebly.com: https://khmerknowledgekeepers.weebly.com/key-featues-of-the-khmer-empire.html.

Kimertimeskh.com. (2024, May 24). *Ninety Years in the Life of Samdech Heng Samrin.* Retrieved from Kimertimeskh.com: https://www.khmertimeskh.com/501494144/ninety-years-in-the-life-of-samdech-heng-samrin/.

Lee, C. J. (2019). *Insurgency: The Cambodian Civil War 1970-1975.* Retrieved from School of Advanced Military Studies: https://apps.dtic.mil/sti/pdfs/AD1083537.pdf.

Leonard C. Overton, D. P. (2025, January 1). *The Decline of Angkor.* Retrieved from Britannica.com: https://www.britannica.com/place/Cambodia/The-decline-of-Angkor.

Library.gov.au. (2022, July 11). *The Decline of the Khmer Empire.* Retrieved from Library.gov.au: https://www.library.gov.au/learn/digital-classroom/angkorkhmer-empire-802-1431/decline-khmer-empire.

Library.gov.au. (2025, January 1). *The Way of Life in the Khmer Empire.* Retrieved from Library.gov.au: https://www.library.gov.au/learn/digital-classroom/angkorkhmer-empire-802-1431/way-life-khmer-empire.

lwmays. (2015, May 21). *Water Technologies of the Khmer Civilization: Angkor.* Retrieved from Ancientwatertechnologies.com: https://ancientwatertechnologies.com/2015/05/21/water-technologies-of-the-khmer-civilization-angkor/.

Michael W. Doyle, I. J. (2009, October 22). *Returning Home: Repatriation of Cambodian Refugees*. Retrieved from Cambridge.org: https://www.cambridge.org/core/books/abs/keeping-the-peace/returning-home-the-repatriation-of-cambodian-refugees/7F2D6C955AB0734D9EBF930D233AEB07.

Miller, M. (2016, January 13). *New Discoveries at Ancient Cambodian Capital Dispel Old Beliefs*. Retrieved from Ancient-origins.net: https://www.ancient-origins.net/news-history-archaeology/new-discoveries-ancient-cambodian-capital-dispel-old-beliefs-005160.

Munez, E. (2024, October 11). *Greater East Asia Co-Prosperity Sphere*. Retrieved from Britannica.com: https://www.britannica.com/topic/Greater-East-Asia-Co-prosperity-Sphere.

Newwoldencyclopedia.org. (2025, January 1). *Khmer Empire*. Retrieved from Newwoldencyclopedia.org: https://www.newworldencyclopedia.org/entry/Khmer_Empire.

Office of the Historian. (1974, August 14). *137. Telegram from the Embassy in Cambodia to the Department of State*. Retrieved from History.state.gov: https://history.state.gov/historicaldocuments/frus1969-76v10/d137.

Osborne, M. (2012, October 18). *The Complex Legacy of Norodom Sihanouk*. Retrieved from Lowryinstitute.org: https://www.lowyinstitute.org/archive/complex-legacy-norodom-sihanouk.

oup.com. (2025, January 1). *The Khmer Empire*. Retrieved from oup.com: https://www.oup.com.au/__data/assets/pdf_file/0024/58191/Chapter-13-The-Khmer-Empire-obook-only.pdf.

Parida, S. (2020, August). *Case Analysis of the Cambodian Elections of 1993 and 1998*. Retrieved from Researchgate.net: https://www.researchgate.net/publication/344202929_Case_Analysis_of_the_Cambodian_Elections_of_1993_and_1998.

Peacekeeping.un.org. (2024, December 28). *Cambodia-UNTAC*. Retrieved from Peacekeeping.un.org: https://peacekeeping.un.org/mission/past/untacbackgr2.html#six.

Plubins, R. Q. (2013, March 12). *Khmer Empire*. Retrieved from Worldhistory.org: https://www.worldhistory.org/Khmer_Empire/.

Prasad, J. (2020, April 14). *Climate Change and the Collapse of Angkor Wat*. Retrieved from Sydney.edu.au: https://www.sydney.edu.au/news-opinion/news/2020/04/14/climate-change-and-angkor-wat-collapse.html.

Rosenberg, J. (2018, August 17). *Tet Offensive*. Retrieved from ThoughtCo.: https://www.thoughtco.com/tet-offensive-vietnam-1779378.

Sailingstonetravel.com. (2018, December 26). *The Mysteries of Jayavarman VII's Triad Temples*. Retrieved from Sailingstone.com:
https://sailingstonetravel.com/jayavarman-viis-triad-temples/.

Strangio, S. (2023, September 19). *Cambodia's Hun Sen: The Tiger That Rules the Mountain*. Retrieved from Thediplomat.com:
https://thediplomat.com/2023/09/cambodias-hun-sen-the-tiger-that-rules-the-mountain/.

Szczepanski, K. (2019, October 16). *What Was French Indochina?* Retrieved from ThoughtCo.com: https://www.thoughtco.com/what-was-french-indochina-195328.

Tourism. (2023, February 2). Retrieved from Opendevelopmentcambodiaa.net:
https://opendevelopmentcambodia.net/topics/tourism/.

Tpocambodia.org. (2024, December 29). *Promoting Healing & Reconciliation Through Psychosocial Interventions*. Retrieved from Tpocambodia.org:
https://tpocambodia.org/promoting-healing-and-reconciliation/.

United States Institute of Peace. (2000, February 22). *Peace Agreements: Cambodia*. Retrieved from Usip.org:
https://www.usip.org/publications/2000/02/peace-agreements-cambodia.

Vachon, M. (2017, April 21). *Healing a Nation*. Retrieved from English.cambodiadailycom: https://english.cambodiadaily.com/features/healing-a-nation-128377/.

Vachon, M. (2023, November 9). *Cambodia's Independence: What It Took to Make This Happen 70th Years Ago*. Retrieved from Cambodianess.com:
https://cambodianess.com/article/cambodias-independence-what-it-took-to-make-this-happen-70th-years-ago.

VanDeCarr, P. (2018, September 30). *How Cambodia Is Clearing Landmines to Rebuild Peace*. Retrieved from Govinsider.asia: https://govinsider.asia/intl-en/article/how-cambodia-is-clearing-landmines-to-rebuild-peace.

Varro, L. (2024, December 1). *Bayon Temple*. Retrieved from Lucasvarro.com: https://lucasvarro.com/blogs/angkorpedia/bayon-temple.

Varro, L. (2024, December 1). *Preah Jhan Temple*. Retrieved from Lucasvarro.com: https://lucasvarro.com/blogs/angkorpedia/preah-khan-temple.

Vietnamtheartofwar.com. (2024, December 18). *25 December 1978: Vietnam Invades Cambodia*. Retrieved from Vietnamtheartofwar.com:
https://vietnamtheartofwar.com/1978/12/01/25-december-1978-vietnam-invades-cambodia/.

William S. Turley, Gerald C. Hickey. (2024, December 3). *The Conquest of Vietnam by France*. Retrieved from Britannica.com:

https://www.britannica.com/place/Vietnam/The-conquest-of-Vietnam-by-France.

Willis, C. C. (2023, October 2). *Protecting Cambodia's Cultural Heritage: US-Cambodia Conservation Ties.* Retrieved from Asiamattersforamerica.org: https://asiamattersforamerica.org/articles/protecting-cambodias-cultural-heritage-us-cambodia-conservation-ties.

World History EDU. (2024, May 26). *History & Major Facts About the Khmer Empire.* Retrieved from Worldhistoryedu.com: https://worldhistoryedu.com/history-major-facts-about-the-khmer-empire/.

Worldbank.org. (2022, November 28). *Cambodia Poverty Assessment 2022: Toward a More Inclusive and Resilient Cambodia.* Retrieved from Worldbank.org: https://www.worldbank.org/en/country/cambodia/publication/cambodia-poverty-assessment-2022-toward-a-more-inclusive-and-resilient-cambodia.

Worldbank.org. (2024, December 29). *Cambodian Agriculture in Transition: Opportunities and Risks.* Retrieved from Worldbank.org: https://www.worldbank.org/en/country/cambodia/publication/cambodian-agriculture-in-transition-opportunities-and-risks.

Yonetici. (2024, August 24). *Bringing History to Life: Educating Cambodian Youth on the Khmer Rouge.* Retrieved from Balert.org: https://balert.org/2024/08/24/bringing-history-to-life-educating-cambodian-youth-on-the-khmer-rouge-genocide/.

Image Sources

1 Tanakorn Srichaisuphakit, CC BY-SA 4.0 <https://creativecommons.org/licenses/by-sa/4.0>, via Wikimedia Commons, https://commons.wikimedia.org/wiki/File:Mainland_Southeast_Asia_in_700_CE_(cropped).png

2 Stefan Fussan, CC BY-SA 3.0 <https://creativecommons.org/licenses/by-sa/3.0>, via Wikimedia Commons, https://commons.wikimedia.org/wiki/File:Preah_Khan_-_House_of_Fire_4425.jpg

3 Jembezmamy, CC0, via Wikimedia Commons, https://commons.wikimedia.org/wiki/File:Map-of-southeast-asia_900_CE.svg

4 Jakub Halun, Attribution-ShareAlike 4.0 International, CC BY-SA 4.0 <https://creativecommons.org/licenses/by-sa/4.0/deed.en> https://commons.wikimedia.org/wiki/File:20171126_Angkor_Wat_4712_DxO.jpg

5 https://commons.wikimedia.org/wiki/File:Cambodia-buddha-11thcentury-fix2.jpg

6 Bearsmalaysia, CC BY-SA 3.0 <https://creativecommons.org/licenses/by-sa/3.0>, via Wikimedia Commons, https://commons.wikimedia.org/wiki/File:French_Indochina_subdivisions.svg

7 https://commons.wikimedia.org/wiki/File:LonNol.jpg

8 https://commons.wikimedia.org/wiki/File:Mao_Sihanouk.jpg

9 Toony, CC BY-SA 3.0 <https://creativecommons.org/licenses/by-sa/3.0>, via Wikimedia Commons, https://commons.wikimedia.org/wiki/File:Khmer_rouge_clothing.jpg

10 https://commons.wikimedia.org/wiki/File:Skulls_from_the_killing_fields.jpg

11 jean-christophe windland, CC BY-SA 3.0 <https://creativecommons.org/licenses/by-sa/3.0>, via Wikimedia Commons, https://commons.wikimedia.org/wiki/File:S-21_cellules.JPG

12 User:BorysMapping, CC BY-SA 4.0 <https://creativecommons.org/licenses/by-sa/4.0>, via Wikimedia Commons, https://commons.wikimedia.org/wiki/File:Vietnamese_invasion_of_Cambodia.png

13 http://fototeca.iiccr.ro/, https://commons.wikimedia.org/wiki/File:Norodom_Sianuc74b_(cropped).jpg

14 World Trade Organization from Switzerland (proccession made by Roman Kubanskiy), CC BY-SA 2.0 <https://creativecommons.org/licenses/by-sa/2.0>, via Wikimedia Commons, https://commons.wikimedia.org/wiki/File:Hun_Sen_July_2019.jpg

www.ingramcontent.com/pod-product-compliance
Lightning Source LLC
Chambersburg PA
CBHW070338010526
44107CB00004B/543